The
GROWTH
Hacking Book

Copyrights

ISBN: 978-1-7330955-5-6

Cover Designed by
A1 Future Technologies Pvt Ltd & Da Light Hub (Ar. Surbhi Jindal)

Formatted by
Vanzzsolutions (weformat)

DEDICATION

Dedicated to all who work passionately crafting their dreams, building their empire and leaving a legacy...

&

Special dedication to our dear friend Santosh Reddy who believed in the project right from the beginning and who is showering his support and love from heaven. We miss you...

ACKNOWLEDGEMENTS

We would like to express our deep and sincere gratitude to all our authors who believed in "The Growth Hacking Book". Thanks to all our contributors for authentically sharing their invaluable insights and best-kept industry secrets in their chapters.

The completion of this resourceful book could not have been possible without the efforts of all the wonderful people whose names may not all be enumerated but their assistance is greatly appreciated.

We would especially like to thank the following friends who have been working tirelessly behind the curtains:

- **Lisa Robbins -** our amazing editor who is always ready to work on last-minute edits with a smile.

- **Evita Ramparte -** our unofficial branding expert for her help in defining the look, vibes and brand of the project.

- **Srish Agrawal -** for offering his company's expertise for designing the cover.

- **Deepak Gupta -** for formatting and layout of the book.

- **Shailendra Mishra -** for his help in inviting dignitaries and VIPs for our launch.

- **Brad Szollose -** for his trust and encouragement in the form of Foreword for the book.

- **Invincible Winners -** our online family of high achievers for their constant support, feedback and encouragement.

We would also like to thank our parents and family members for their support, patience and dealing with our crazy schedules as we burnt the midnight oil while working on this book.

Above all, thanks to the Great Almighty, the author of knowledge and wisdom for showering his love and countless blessings.

To the "Growth Hacking and Marketing" community for their moral, financial and physical support - thank you!

"It truly takes a village to build a dream, raise an empire."

Sincerely,

Parul Agrawal & Rohan Chaubey
Compilers of "The Growth Hacking Book"
Founders, Growth Media AI
www.growthmedia.ai

FOREWORD

By Brad Szollose

───◆───

It is the 21st century. We find ourselves living in a digital space. Our eyes are scanning hundreds of Internet pages a day. Our attention span is reduced to that of a couple of seconds. What is it that determines whether your brain and eye-balls will pay attention to this page over the other one? Whose message will get across? Which product or service will catch on and become a billion-dollar brand? Which movie will be the new blockbuster? What determines this or that content to appear in front of us at all?

The traditional marketing and digital marketing are overexploited. To get the results very few people get, you have to do what very few are willing to do. Silicon Valley's 'secret sauce' is now revealed - Growth Hacking and Growth Hackers!

They are behind the viral spread of likes, comments, and shares on social media. They are the wizards behind the trends and movements. They work backstage behind mega events and top-paid celebrities. They are behind everything you see, buy, hear, watch - and they are behind the fact that you are looking at all!

This book removes the curtain. Growth Marketers get to come forward on the stage; they get to speak; they get to be the voice and enjoy the spotlight. Those ingenious, hard-working, tech wizards - sometimes of young age - genuinely deserve the credit. We owe them respect for they are pushing boundaries and showing us the possibilities.

In this book, you get to learn from them directly. Growth Hackers are stepping forward to empower you. Whether you are an author, coach, marketer, consultant or entrepreneur - you will find their growth hacking secrets priceless. Now, you can learn from them, download their magic, install their mindset, and scale your growth using their tools.

The ideas shared in this book aren't just for startups. They are relevant for big corporates and personal brands as well. The practical tips shared in the book are underused and lesser-known; time to act is now if you want to get an edge in the market!

The slower pace of the past is long gone. It is now possible to scale businesses faster than ever using growth hacking framework. The companies that have hacked their growth are revealing everything they know.

The marketing insights you're about to explore and powerful tools you're about to gain will truly transform the way startups and companies approach marketing and growth.

I am honored to introduce this book, and the authors within, to you.

Warmly,
Brad Szollose
Leader. Visionary. Author of Liquid Leadership
The Host of Awakened Nation
www.bradszollose.com

THE GROWTH HACKING BOOK
INTRODUCTION

By Rohan Chaubey

Imagine how it would feel if every time you launched a product, published content, or offered services, you get an overwhelming response from your target audience.

Everything you touch turns to gold.

You built an engine to achieve product-market fit.

You get overbooked even before the launch — no questions asked.

This book will show you how.

Prerequisite for Growth Hacking

The prerequisite to hack growth is to understand that growth hacking is not a pipedream or a silver bullet.

Aren't we tired of hearing so-called "experts" telling us:

- A one-trick pony that can make everything better
- If you do this one thing your startup will become a billion-dollar company
- No time or effort required, acquire paying customers while you're sleeping

I don't believe it.

Growth Hacking requires hard work.

Instead of asking, "Will this work?", ask yourself, "Are you willing to put in the work to make it work?"

Growth Hacking is not magic. There are no shortcuts.

Growth Hackers do things that maybe traditional marketers wouldn't think about doing.

If you're reading this, I bet you are someone who thinks differently; you're not afraid to take the unconventional path to growth.

All that's required of you is a willingness to think about growth and marketing in a different way than you're probably used to.

I encourage you to take action on the information in this book if you truly want to unlock explosive, exponential and long-term growth.

This book is for: Founders, Entrepreneurs, CMOs, Growth Hackers, Growth Marketers, Growth Engineers, Growth Leads, Product Marketers, Data Scientists, or anyone working to grow a startup or a business brand or a personal brand.

What is Growth Hacking?

Growth Hacking is conducting marketing experiments to uncover strategies to acquire and retain customers/users using data.

It can be anything - viral marketing, publicity stunts, leveraging trends or other people's audience, inbound/outbound/automated, copywriting, gamification, etc. The possibilities are infinite.

A growth hacker is someone that operates at the intersection of product, marketing, and technology to methodically acquire, activate and retain users/followers/clients.

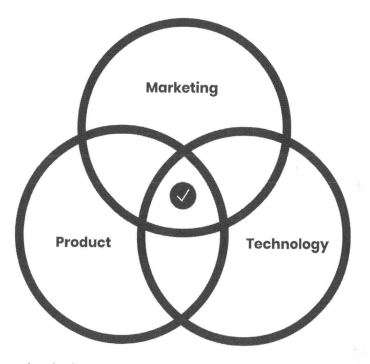

www.rohanchaubey.com

1. **Marketing**: Growth Hacker uses inbound and outbound strategies to attract traffic.

2. **Technology**: Sometimes, growth is achieved by building growth tools. It is not necessary for growth hackers to be a coder, but a growth hacker should be able to write pseudocode to implement code-heavy solutions.

3. **Product**: Product level decisions are used to activate and retain people. Example - UI/UX, gamification, copywriting, referral system within the product, etc.

Don't let other self-proclaimed experts, gurus, ninjas, etc. hypnotize you into thinking that you do not have the power to define Growth Hacking. There are no boundaries. Don't let them box you into their idea of what Growth Hacking should be.

There is a negative connotation to the word "Hacking" because we all hate hackers that steal our private data, money or identity.

However, Growth Hacking is different. Growth Hackers are not black hat hackers.

Growth hacking is not hacking in a literal sense. Growth Hackers do not adopt fraudulent means to grow a business.

A growth hack is an unconventional + creative approach to marketing a startup.

What is your job as a Growth Hacker?

Your job as a Growth Hacker is to experiment and discover "measurable + scalable + repeatable" process to grow an important metric (North Star Metric) for a business.

Once you find a proven process that delivers predictable results, you either try to automate it or someone on the marketing team executes it.

Difference between a growth hacker and a digital marketer is that the growth hackers work at all stages of the AARRR (Acquisition, Activation, Retention, Referral, Revenue) funnel.

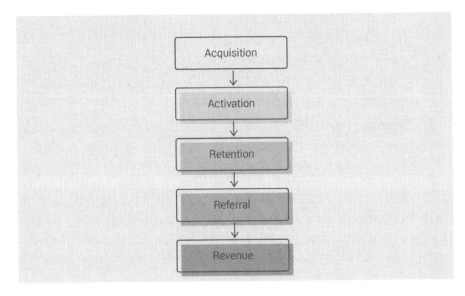

The goal of the growth hacker is to move the website visitors down the funnel.

1. Acquisition - Generating awareness and targeted traffic to your website.

2. Activation - Turning casual visitors into users.

3. Retention - Making users come back and keep them as long-term users.

4. Referral - Users recommending your product to others.

5. Revenue - Turning users into paid customers. The revenue stage can come before or after the referral stage.

Funnel Stage	Growth Tactics
Acquisition	**1. Inbound (Pull Tactics) -** **1.1 Your Audience:** Blogging, SEO, Podcasting, Social Media, E-Books, Webinars, Guides, Whitepaper, Infographics, Videos/YouTube, Slide Decks, Contests **1.2 Leveraged Audience**: Guest Blogging, Guest Podcasting, Speaking at Conferences, Guest Hosting Webinars, Deal Sites, Marketplaces **2. Outbound (Push Tactics)** - Affiliates, Direct Sales. Paid Ads, Promotional Swaps **3. Automation** - Network Invitations (Phone Contacts, Email Contacts, Social Contacts), Social Sharing, API Integrations

Activation	Landing Pages, Copywriting, CTAs, Onboarding, Gamification, Social Proof, Pricing (Tiers, Discrimination, Naming, Trials, Freemium, Discounts, Riskless)
Retention	Email, Alerts and Notifications, UI/UX, Exit Interviews, Increase Value, Community Building

*The above list is suggestive, not exhaustive.

Example 1. Inbound Pull Tactic (E-Book): A New York-based SaaS company was aiming to acquire 1000+ beta users. I created a lead magnet as a bribe for their audience. It was designed to go viral on LinkedIn. By posting one LinkedIn update on my profile, the company acquired 1000+ leads within a week. That's the power of reserve engineering content production and distribution.

Example 2. Automation Tactic using API Integration: Our clients wanted to grow bigger than their competitors on Twitter, so we developed a SaaS platform that used a special algorithm and underutilized Twitter APIs for crazy free organic reach.

Example 3: Inbound Pull Tactic (Leveraged Audience): Leveraging other people's network is also a growth hack! It is easier to hijack other people's audience than to build yours from scratch. A lot of SaaS companies try to partner with me to market to my 250000+ followers that I have grown organically over the years.

I shared the above examples to convey that a growth hack can be anything. Do not subscribe to other people's definition of what a growth hack is supposed to be.

Feel free to experiment with any growth channel. Don't be restricted to social media and SEO.

Growth Hacking is finding untraditional ways to grow a product or service, through the use of data, technology and sometimes a system's weakness exploitation.

What do you need to do to become a Growth Hacker?

It doesn't require any special qualifications to be a growth hacker. All you need is a growth mindset. Anyone can learn growth marketing.

1. Spend time reading about Growth Hacking as much as you can!

- Take notes. Record the best ideas you have read.
- Put knowledge into action. Everything you do should be testable, trackable and scalable.

2. Find someone who has "been there and done that."

- Look for mentors.
- Growth hacking is methodical. Learn about their secrets strategies, tools, tactics, framework, processes, etc.
- RohanChaubeyTV is a web television show for entrepreneurs and growth marketers to learn everything about growth. Learn from the industry leaders and get certified by taking the growth hacking course for free.

3. Cultivate Growth Hacking Mindset.

- Leverage other people's time, money, talents and network. I hire my friends, students and contacts from my professional network.
- Leverage the power of scalable tools. Look for trends, patterns and ways to optimize and automate.
- The "secret" is the mindset, not the toolset.

4. Experiment and find your own Growth Hacking Techniques.

- I did not want to spend money on Twitter advertising, so I built a SaaS platform that helps brands and influencers hack the Twitter algorithm for crazy free organic reach!

- My latest LinkedIn update went viral organically with 330,000 views and 1000+ comments. Ever since then, I have been approached by many companies and C-level executives to get my help in achieving the same.

- Instagram crossed 1 Billion users milestone. I get many inquiries from brands to grow on Instagram. So we developed a tool that can help influencers and brands grow their Instagram reach organically + exponentially by exploiting the IG features and algorithm.

- Instagram doesn't have a friendly interface to access the contact information of your followers or influencers. So we developed a tool that helps you get the contact information of any Instagram account from a pool of 25 million business accounts.

5. Understand marketing and analytics.

- Know the rules to bend them to your will.

- Harness the power of analytics. Conclude based on data, not instinct.

- Always be learning.

Three Untold Truths about Growth

#1. Growth Hacking is an infinite game: Bad products (products that don't create real value) can succeed (sales-wise) because of great marketing. However, growth will be short-term. Remember fads like Fidget spinner?

The opposite is also true — great products can fail because of poor marketing.

Growth is never bound to happen; you make it happen. That's why you need a growth marketer to approach growth strategically.

Invest in growth marketing for the businesses that aim to stand the test of time. Of course, you can iterate until you achieve product-market fit.

Growth Hacking is an infinite game which you continue playing until there is a need for your product in the market; even if all the players (competitors) drop out, you keep playing.

#2. Virality or Growth is never accidental: Viral and growth are always orchestrated or provoked. It never happens by a twist of fate.

Growth is never by mere chance; it is the result of forces working together.

#3. Kings of hype get overbooked even before the launch: Ever wondered why every Apple launch is massively hyped? Because they are thinking of growth and distribution even before the product launches.

Growth marketing should begin months or even a year before the product launch.

Most startups fail because they focus only on the product and think about "growth" after the product launch. If you believe in the value that your product will create, there's no reason to wait until the product launch to start selling it.

There's a reason vapourware get more media attention than product launch events.

The 5-Step Framework for Growth Hacking Success

Step 1: Pin down your North Star metric (NSM).

Definition of NSM - The North Star Metric is the single metric that best captures the core value that your product delivers to customers. - Sean Ellis

Example of an NSM (North Star Metric):
Quora (Online Community)
Core value = Facilitate the sharing of knowledge in the world
North Star Metric = Number of questions answered

Step 2: Build a Growth Model.

Build apps/products/services so valuable that businesses have no choice but to buy your solution!

Product + Marketing = Growth

Step 3: Produce a strategy. Formulate action steps (tactics) building mini models. Tactics are short-term; the strategy is long-term.

A list of growth tactics is shared earlier in this chapter.

Step 4: Implement in a timely, regular scheduled way before you Monitor. Pay keen attention to your progress and adjust until you get what you want. Iteration is the key.

Step 5: Focus on benefitting and serving others (Check Step 2 - Value Delivery)

If you follow the above five steps, the world is your oyster.

GrowthSet

To become a world-class growth hacker, you have to work on your GrowthSet relentlessly. In this book, we define GrowthSet using a mathematical formula.

GrowthSet = Skillset + Mindset + Toolset

www.rohanchaubey.com

The following chapters are categorized into three sets (Skillset, Mindset and Toolset) each helping you become a better entrepreneur and a growth marketer.

About Rohan

Rohan is one of the most followed Growth Hackers. Learn one growth hack every day at RohanChaubey.com

TABLE OF CONTENTS

Skillset **1**

Content Skillset **2**

How To Leverage Content That Will Take Your Brand
To The Moon

By Manish Nepal 3

How To Start And Scale Your Online Magazine

By Dillon Kivo 16

Great Content Needs a Great Writer, a Purpose,
and the Right Approach

By Issac Thomas 25

Building Marketing Assets That Appreciate
In Value While Generating a Modest Income
for Many Years to Come

By Dennis Langlais 33

Essential SEO Growth Hacks — Learn to
Rank your Site Faster

By Surabh Tiwari 43

Grabbing Media Attention To
Grow Your Personal Brand

By Deepak V. Maddila 51

How To Pitch Journalists For Public Relations Success

By Rahul Singh 61

Social Media Skills 69

Growth Hacking Your Presence On Linkedin
And Making An Impact

By Yaagneshwaran Ganesh 70

Influencer Marketing: Getting Results Via
A Data Driven Process

By Ishaan Shakunt 81

Instagram Growth: 0 To 10K Followers In 3 Months

By Vivek Agrawal 96

Tactical Skills 105

The Science Of Writing A Bestselling Book

By Parul Agrawal 106

A Bird In The Hand: Is Paying Attention
Your Greatest Growth Hack?

By Suneet Bhatt 116

The Power Of Customer Retention

by Arun Kumar Sharma 127

Growing Business in an Unorthodox Niche 143

Growth Hack Your Food Business
Through Digital Marketing

By Nitish Mathur 144

Backstage Secrets To Grow Your Business
In The Music Industry

By Christian Fictoor 151

Growing Your Brick and Mortar Business in
The Digital Era

By Priya Kalra 159

Growth Hacking The Newsjacking Way

By Srish Agrawal 163

How To Brand Leverage Offline Marketing
For Audience Growth

By S. Shiva SriCharan 174

Online Success Secrets For Health And
Wellness Practitioners, Coaches And Consultants

By Lisa Robbins 183

Mindset **191**

Bend The Reality Of Networking

By Ruchi G. Kalra 192

Leveraging The Power Of Relationships
To Grow Your Online Business

By Kelisha Mills 198

Using OKR Strategy For Success
In Business

By Shailendra Mishra 206

Guideline To Become A Successful
Digital Entrepreneur

By Badr Berrada 212

How To Create Financial Growth By
Being Your Fearless Self

By Noam Kostucki 221

Build A Celebrity Brand & Raise
An Army Of Light

By Evita Ramparte 228

Toolset **235**

The Ultimate Guide On Generating Leads
Via Cold Email

By Will Cannon 236

How To Create An Army Of 1000 Micro-Influencers
In 30 Days Who Will Sell For You

By Deep Kakkad 245

Automate Workflows To Make Growth
Hacking Easy

By Rachit Khator 252

Why Partnerships Are The Ultimate
Growth Hack

By Naser Alubaidi 264

How To Market Your Business
Like A Reality Tv Show:

Harnessing The Power Of Storytelling To Make
Money And Grow Your Business

By Tim Wasmundt 274

Growth Hacks To Generate A Flood of Leads,
Customers and Profits (Without Paid Ads)

By Rohan Chaubey and Amit Kumar 281

About the Publisher: **295**

SKILLSET

Learn how to attract, activate and retain clients/users/followers.

CONTENT SKILLSET

"Content is the reason search
began in the first place."

LEE ODDEN

HOW TO LEVERAGE CONTENT THAT WILL TAKE YOUR BRAND TO THE MOON

By Manish Nepal

———◆———

Growth hacking content is not rocket science. You can just apply the following most common hacks to attract traffic to your content pages:

1. Identify the high-volume SEO keywords in your product domain.

2. Write 3–5 keywords-based articles per week. Use the Skyscraper Technique to outrank your competitors.

3. Respond to relevant questions on Quora and post blog snippets on other relevant communities to build backlinks.

4. Nudge your colleagues to upvote your posts (from multiple accounts) in forums and communities every time you publish a new blog.

5. Promote your blogs by scheduling social media posts on Sundays at 7 pm, Wednesdays at 9 am, and Thursdays between 12-2 pm — the most popular "me-time" for content consumers.

6. Repurpose your content for podcasts, YouTube, SlideShare, or other leading content syndication platforms.

7. Apply "newsjacking" technique to earn explosive traffic to your blog site.

I have seen multiple content teams applying the above hacks to their content marketing strategy and succeed — albeit only for the short run. But I'm not going to recommend this to you because it's a hamster treadmill that will tire you out soon and won't lead you anywhere.

You picked up this book because you want to build a successful brand. Among other valuable ideas that you will read about in other chapters of this book, creating content for your brand is a critical and sustainable strategy to achieve that goal.

But there's no shortcut to creating great content that is going to be a smashing overnight hit. Growth hacking content limits the scope of your content to SEO writing and shallow readership. It's not a great way to build a monumental cathedral that lives on for hundreds of years.

"If your brand is a cathedral you are building, each piece of content you produce is the perfectly-chiseled stone that gives shape and foundation to your brand's edifice. #TheGrowthHackingBook

In this chapter, I offer suggestions to replace the flash-in-the-pan content marketing hacks with a reliable seven-step strategy to amplify your brand's growth.

Building a rock solid content strategy

A good content strategy requires you to follow a religious ritual of putting out great content that will earn you multiple benefits such as brand awareness, lead conversions, and continuous growth. Depending on where your brand is right now in your growth plan, you can apply the following tips to better strategize your content marketing:

1. Set hard goals

The reasons most brands create content is because:

- They want to maintain their presence through blogging.
- They think Google ranks new content higher.
- It's what everyone else is doing.

Look closer and you will see that it's a very purposeless strategy to have. If you're creating content for the sake of remaining an active brand, you will end up stockpiling an archive of lifeless content that will die a lonely death.

Set a high standard for your content strategy. Start by creating clear, measurable goals and timelines. It can also become to be a self-fulfilling prophecy for your brand if you articulate your goals in the most vivid details. For a bootstrapping startup, for example, your goals can read something like this:

> *"We want our blog to be read by 1,000,000 people by the end of 2022. We want 15 people to subscribe each week within the first two years and 150+ subscribers per week during the following two years."*

Your brand's content should have a purpose, a meaning to live up to, a cause to rally for. Set goals that will keep your content team accountable.

Set a goal to earn a respectable blog subscription following within a realistic timeline.

Aim for meaningful traffic to your blogs from relevant demographics.

Hold your content team up against a variable lead quota every month.

2. Identify overarching themes

Every product represents a value or stands for some cause:

- Slack is a team collaboration tool; their content extols the importance of workplace productivity.

- General Electric is a technology conglomerate; they write blogs extensively on robotics, the global economy, and public policy.

- Tom Bilyeu hosts Impact Theory, an interview series where he invites the world's greatest achievers to talk about living a fulfilled life.

Your content should be a reflection of the belief that your products and services advocate. It should inspire thought-provoking ideas that align with your brand and communicates the vision you have for the world. Identifying the overarching themes for your content is more important than writing blog posts based on high-volume search keywords.

(Image source: author. Designed with spark.adobe.com)

3. Hire the right ~~copywriters~~ people

It's no secret that great content teams are made up of great copywriters. But copywriters are generalists at best. Sometimes, you need to dig deep and find domain specialists who can become your brand ambassadors.

You need marketers that live and breathe your product or service and who are able to clearly communicate its value to the world. Look beyond hiring grammar gurus and punctuation pundits for your content team; hire passionate storytellers who can humanize your brand.

But what if you are bootstrapping and don't have money lying around to hire a stellar content personality? Don't worry. You can either identify in-house champions, such as one of the co-founders or the product managers, who are good at telling stories. On top of my head, two names that exemplify this strategy are Naval Ravikant (of AngelList) and Sahil Lavingia (of Gumroad).

I've seen this many times over in my 7+ years of content marketing profession: the best storytellers in an organization aren't necessarily the writers; it's usually the unsuspecting people in your business who understand the product ecosystem better than most. They are diamonds in the rough and their story and narrative can be great assets to your marketing team. They don't necessarily have to bust their backs to "write" content full-time; they can dictate their ideas that trained copywriters can spin into marketable tales.

You can also partner with emerging experts in your field who can represent your ideas and give them the bully pulpit to speak on topics closer to your brand. It's a mutual win for both parties.

4. Stick to your niche

A common trap most businesses fall for on their path to growth is the temptation to be the next Procter & Gamble. But unlike trying to sell the sundry consumer goods, your content should cater specifically to your niche audience. Build your buyer persona and stick to content that they want to read.

Resist the temptation to make love to the entire world. When you try to offer something to everyone, your content becomes a reference book rather than a reliable source of information.

Here's a simple example to drive this point home. The US has over 7,000 magazines published every year. These magazines cater to more than 36 different demographics. Thousands of these publications compete for the same audience because of their overlapping interests. The majority of them run on profits; they are constantly looking for ways to expand their digital footprint and maximize revenue.

The magazines share the profit pie even in such a competitive space because they specialize in writing for their targeted audience. The editors of *Elle* are better off nurturing their readers for a three-year magazine subscription rather than trying to convert *The Chronicle* readers because of how alien the interests of the latter group are.

Apply the same principle to your content strategy and you will ensure a steep growth in readership and traffic within the first few months of your strategizing. Make your content special for one demography; don't make it an assorted library of miscellaneous for everyone walking on the street.

5. Set an infallible cadence

Your content is your brand's mouthpiece. Once you pick the proverbial bullhorn and start speaking to your audience, you have to live up to their expectations. Being erratic in your publication schedule breaches an unspoken promise and makes your business look frivolous.

Create a realistic content calendar and stay true to your schedule without fail. Don't fall for the myth that says you have to publish 30 content pieces per month. Do what's within your means and give it depth. But deliver on the promise of consistency and quality.

Every content out there in the online world is vying for an average person's attention, like Tinder matches. Most of your audience have a

4X3 mobile screen and a few fleeting seconds to decide which content to consume and which ones to skip. In essence, your content is competing against the high-flying suitors such as *The New Yorker*, *Harvard Business Review*, and *The Huffington Post*. If your content doesn't catch your audience's fancy or is not up to the mark, they will left-swipe your content to oblivion, so to speak.

To avoid this from happening, produce the most riveting, evergreen content in the industry and do so as a brand ritual. Setting a cadence to your content creation and distribution lets your audience anchor on to your brand stories amidst the overwhelming content noise.

6. Build a content funnel

A big question that your brand and content creators should ask is — how is content going to help your business grow? The simple answer is, once you have all the moving parts in place, it's pretty easy to attract leads and improve sales. Tactically speaking, you need to create a content funnel to convert leads.

Write meaningful content that strikes a chord with customers who are at different stages of the buying journey. Get help from SEO experts; they can break down the long-tail search keywords that consumers are looking for so that you can address these search queries in your content.

You can also funnel your content pieces so your audience can discover posts that are relevant to them. HubSpot does it wonderfully for almost every major topic related to marketing. Just type any marketing-related keyword into Google and you'll likely find a HubSpot blog post written about it.

Here's an example:

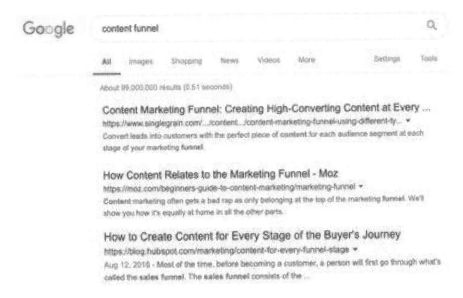

It's no accident that all of these top-of-the-funnel pages have a lead magnet content somewhere in the post. The lead magnet, often a downloadable (and irresistible) content assent, offers deeper-level insights that are relevant to what's covered in the blog post. When I finished reading the blog post, here's what I saw placed strategically at the end of the post:

This lead magnet is super relevant to my internet search for content funnels, so I naturally click on the download banner and land on the sign-up page:

HubSpot

NORTH AMERICA
888 482 7768

FREE DOWNLOAD: CONTENT MAPPING TEMPLATE

Learn how to use buyer personas and lifecycle stages to create targeted content.

Creating relevant, valuable content is a major tenet of inbound marketing. The content you're creating should be in line with the goals and challenges of specific segments of your audience.

It all boils down to: You need to create the right content, for the right people, at the right time. And the best way to do that? Through mapping out your content according to buyer persona and lifecycle stage.

Sound a bit complicated? Don't worry! We've created a content mapping template that will walk you through the entire process.

You'll learn how to:

- Understand buyer personas and lifecycle stages

I want to download this!

First Name *

Last Name *

Email *

Phone Number *

Company Name *

How many employees work there? *

Therein begins my journey of being a HubSpot customer. Since they now have my email address, they will send me the promised content and nurture me with more relevant, bottom-of-the-funnel content to try and convert me as a customer — given I'm the right buyer persona.

This is a longer but proven strategy that encapsulates the entire buyer journey by dovetailing different content pieces in a seamless progression. But in one of my recent interviews with Tim Soulo, Chief Marketing Officer for Ahrefs.com, shared a shorter way to create a content funnel.

Here is his slightly paraphrased quote when I asked about the import of creating content for customers at different stages of the buy

"I'm not a big advocate of creating a customer journey. I believe that when someone searches for a solution to a problem and lands on your page, you have an opportunity to make that person go through the entire journey right on that page. You don't need to send them to different pieces of content. You can explain about the problem, where it comes from, and explain the different remedy options. Then, on that same page, you can say that a particular solution is not reliable because it works for some, but not for others."

I love the simplicity of his idea. It's an immensely overlooked strategy in content marketing. Your content needs depth to be able to cater to all stages of a customer journey, but it's a worthy endeavor that offers many advantages.

The value of creating specialized, long-form content becomes more pronounced here. Evergreen, long-form content for your business can withstand the test of time. Even Google rewards longer content over short, keyword-stuffed blog posts.

7. Double down on distribution

Nothing can compensate for bad content — not even the greatest marketing gimmicks. However, most brands fail in their content marketing not because they have bad content but because they lack a good distribution strategy. A well-thought-out promotion strategy is the best bedfellow for a great quality content.

The best way to promote your content is to build an email list of subscribers and notify them every time you put out a new piece of content. Don't believe anyone who says email is dead. It's still the most effective way to grow your community.

Let's look at a simple example to understand the power of email in the content distribution process.

With more than 200 million downloads out of just 350 episodes for the Tim Ferriss Show podcast, Tim is the undisputed *Oprah of Audio*. His blog, which existed before he began his podcast journey, gets over a million visitors every month. For most individual brands, that's a lucrative empire that they can live off of forever. But Tim doesn't sit on his laurels. He knows that in today's volatile economy, if you're out of your readers' sight, pretty soon you're going to be out of their minds.

He has a subscription option for his blog to increase reader returns for the new content he puts out. On top of that, he heavily promotes *5-Bullet Friday*, a weekly newsletter exclusive to the people who've subscribed to it.

His blog subscribers get notified about his latest podcast every time a new episode comes out. Similarly, the 5-Bullet Friday newsletter highlights and links to the latest podcast episode in every edition. This way, Tim not only attracts new readers to his blogs and podcasts, he retains them solely through email.

There are different channels that work effectively for different brands. Social media is a great way to promote your content, but it's not for everyone. Tim Ferriss has more than 949,000 followers on Facebook and 1.59 million followers on Twitter. And yet, his social media engagement is tepid compared to his high-octane emails.

Identify what's great for your brand and stick to that channel for marketing your content. Quora is great for making your content discoverable and getting more traffic to your blog. YouTube is the best when it comes to brand visibility. LinkedIn is effective for personal brand building but not so much for content marketing.

Every great process ends with monitoring and optimizing mechanism. Measure the performance of your content pieces with a tool such as Google Analytics to fix content gaps and refine your process. Monitor where most of your traffic comes from, which content pieces are doing well, how much time your readers spend on your pages, and so on. Emphasize your content production and distribution process based on these findings without getting too caught up in the vanity numbers.

Reach for the moon

Growth hacking is often a very misunderstood concept. Marketers nowadays abuse it to game the system or get short spurts of supposed growth. But there's no genuine value in carrying out such cheap thrills, especially in content. Content is fundamentally a pillar of growth and you need to put in the required hard work to build that pillar. The true spirit of growth hacking lies in coming up with pragmatic ideas that go against the established norms.

In addition to the ideas outlined above, feel free to experiment with new ideas that come to mind. Don't simply use the hacks and tricks that worked for others because what works for them may not work for you. There's no one path to success; the world is your oyster to explore — chart your own course to success.

Author Biography

Manish Nepal is a content marketer, researcher, and co-host of Coffee Conversations a marketing-led LinkedIn video series. He consults up and coming startups on how to look beyond the noise in order to create a sustainable content marketing strategy.

Manish believes that growth-focussed content can help fledgling businesses carve a niche of their own and uplift their marketing game. Manish's original and ghost-written pieces have appeared in prominent publications such as Huffington Post, Forbes, and Entrepreneur.com.

Where to Find Manish
linkedin.com/in/manishnepal
twitter.com/manishood
medium.com/@manishood

Treat your content like a product.
You have to produce, package, and
present viable content and ship it to the
right consumers.

HOW TO START AND SCALE YOUR ONLINE MAGAZINE

By Dillon Kivo

I'd just finished my normal day's tasks: Handling client projects, engaging with my audience on social media, prospecting for more clients, pitching authoritative bloggers in my industry, promoting my guest posts, and a host of other tasks that are typical of an internet entrepreneur in the digital marketing industry.

March 2018, one chilly Tuesday evening as I was winding down after a long and successful day's work and reading an article on Inc.com, an idea occurred to me.

"How about starting my own online magazine?"

Kivo Daily is a business and entrepreneurship online magazine dedicated to serving digital startup founders with practical solutions to accelerate their growth.

In this chapter, I'll show you how to start and scale your own online magazine without breaking the bank or losing your mind in the process. First, let's start with the most important question: Why an online magazine?

Why Should You Start an Online Magazine?

Well, like any other business, starting an online magazine isn't easy.

When you begin to talk about your new project, your friends and family might try to talk you out of it. I was told, "It's such a time-consuming and money-sucking enterprise. Don't do it." Every business is difficult to build, but the truth is, getting an online magazine off the ground is not as difficult as you may think.

I would say that an online magazine is difficult to manage. I can also say that it's actually simple to start. There's a reason more and more people are going into magazine publication.

There are 20,000 consumer and trade publications in North America alone, according to the National Directory of Magazines, and 1,000 new magazines are launched every year! If you have great leadership and management skills, you can build an impressive magazine that will help you make great money for yourself.

Another reason you should build your own online magazine is because people love them. The interest is already there. With the rise of the Internet and mobile phones, more and more people of all ages are reading news and author opinion content from their favorite online magazines rather than from print media. People have turned into digital content consumers.

Of course, the challenge many publishers face is how to get readers to their digital magazine regularly. To do this, you have to give your readers what they want. As Zig Ziglar puts it beautifully:

> *"You can have everything in life you want if you will just help other people get what they want." – Zig Ziglar*

Consequently, catering to your audience should be your main source of motivation. If you tailor your energy around your audience's needs, desires, goals and pain points, I believe you can create a very successful online publication.

My own magazine, Kivo Daily, was actually born out of my desire to serve my audience and offer them valuable content. I wanted to provide a platform where entrepreneurs could share their visions and goals without having to jump through the hurdles of trying to climb what I call "the publication ladder," which are a series of steps that bloggers and publishers need to take before they finally get featured in top tier publications like Forbes, Entrepreneur and CNN.

Essentially, I wanted to give everyone an equal opportunity to offer their solutions, successes and failures so others could learn from them. That's what the Kivo Daily is about, and the comments and results we're getting from our readers have proven to us that we're on the right track.

Your biggest priority shouldn't be your domain name, a microphone or the musical jingle you'll use in your opening. Your biggest priority should be the topics you'll cover. #TheGrowthHackingBook #GrowthHackingMovement #GrowthHackingDay"

Once you've done your research about launching your own online magazine, you need to take next steps:

Step 1: Pick a niche that you're passionate about

Your biggest priority shouldn't be your domain name, a microphone or the musical jingle you'll use in your opening. Your biggest priority should be the topics you'll cover.

A lot of folks make the mistake of picking the wrong topic. Just because a successful publisher has picked, 'LA celebrity news' as their topic and they're killing it, doesn't mean it's the right topic for you. That's the wrong approach to picking a niche. That particular publisher might be passionate about Los Angeles and celebrity news and that's the reason why they chose that niche.

The best thing to do is to focus on covering what you love. Pick a niche you're passionate about, that way, you'll never run out of ideas. You'll always feed your readers compelling content that informs and entertains.

For example, I chose business, entrepreneurship and technology for my online magazine because I love those topics. These are the topics I'm always reading about. I'm an entrepreneur, so I love entrepreneurship stories. This makes me knowledgeable about my niche and helps me publish the best content in the business and entrepreneurship niche and in turn, makes Kivo Daily readers flock to the site to consume and share my stories.

Step 2: Content is the only currency you need

You might think to build your own media company you'll need a lot of start-up capital. Well, you don't need huge sums of money to start your digital publishing company. One of the fundamental lessons I learned from running Kivo Daily is this: Money is secondary when it comes to creating your online magazine.

Great content is really the king of online publishing. It's the only currency you'll need to grow your media empire. Your primary focus should be your content. Simply put, content is the fuel that will power your magazine.

Not just any content: superior quality and valuable content that educates and entertains, and captivating posts that touch readers on an emotional level. I don't care about appealing to advertisers or making more profit. I prefer to publish valuable articles that solve my audience's problems and answer their questions.

I remember how people pressed me to monetize Kivo Daily when I started getting traction. I didn't succumb to this pressure because I knew that the content would bring in a steady flow of readers and those readers would spread the word about my digital publication and bring in the money.

My strategy, even before I launched the Kivo Daily, was to have about 20 high quality articles ready for publication. I published them all at once on the very day I launched the site and I recommend you do the same.

Having between 10 to 20 articles on your site will give you credibility from day one. This will also help your magazine do well on search engines and establish your site as authority in your niche, all from the start!

Step 3: Launch a minimum viable magazine

You don't have to wait. You have to move fast.

Concentrate on getting your first 30-40 posts published, don't worry about having a perfect website with expensive web design, custom landing pages, or fancy writing from a pricey copywriting agency. Just launch a minimum viable magazine or prototype that offers the features that your ideal readers crave.

That's exactly how I launched Kivo Daily, very lean, without injecting huge amounts of money into it. Here's how I did it:

- I bought my domain name for $12.

- Created a WordPress based website for free. I did have to pay for hosting. If you don't know how to create a website you can always outsource that task for around $2,000.

- I wrote a few articles, bought more from freelancers and asked others to contribute, which cost me $250.

That's all it took to launch Kivo Daily. I didn't invest lots of money. I built it based on a lean startup philosophy.

Launching your media company this way will allow you to start your business fast and generate quick feedback from your readers that will help you test your ideas. It will also help you measure and scale your magazine to the next level.

Step 4: To scale, partner with professional freelancers and content creators

It can make sense to grow your digital magazine by spending money on advertising, but I really don't recommend that strategy. I also don't recommend that you look for funding from an investor either. The smart way to go and the way many editors have grown their readership, is to partner, not invest, with smart, professional content creators in a similar, relevant niche.

Brian Clark, the founder and CEO of CopyBlogger Media, the digital marketing magazine that some industry insiders call the 'Bible of Content Marketing,' bootstrapped his business with $1000 and partnered with Darren Rowse, the founder and CEO of ProBlogger, to share each other's articles through guest posting. The word guest posting was not known when they started their businesses.

I used the same strategy with my own online publishing business:

- I bootstrapped Kivo Daily with the money I earned from my digital marketing business.
- I identified who my stakeholders were.
- Finally, I pitched my stakeholders and the rest is history.

Money matters less in this endeavor. You need to partner more with your stakeholders.

That's why, as a magazine publisher, your uttermost priority is to identify your stakeholders, which will include:

- Freelancers — they'll contribute articles to your site.
- Bloggers — you partner with them to guest post on each other's site and gain traffic and traction.

- Content marketers — you network with them. In the end, they'll help promote your site through white label SEO techniques.

- Influencers in your industry — they'll help publicize your magazine with their thousands or millions of fans.

You'll need to strategize and work hard to build a mutual and long-term connection with your stakeholders. I recommend you hire professional freelancers and editors to help you with this!

For me, partnering with stakeholders was more important than anything else, that's why I partnered with freelance writers. I don't care about the country or region a writer comes from. I care about the ideas they bring to the table. I have contributors from all over the world who are pitching different business stories to inspire Kivo Daily readers and I always make sure their content passes my guidelines, or what I call my "quality test" before publishing them.

Conclusion

In my opinion, you've got to join this lucrative industry. You have to be a publisher. You have got to own your digital media company. Not to use as an avenue to engage with your audience or as a medium to feed your customers with great content, building your own magazine is much more than that. It's about creating a media asset that pumps cash and generates tons of fans and leads for you.

Before that chilly Tuesday evening in 2018, I dared to think of building my own online magazine. I'd read content from Forbes and Fast Company and I thought; "this is for the big guys, it's not for me."

Seeing how difficult it was to pitch to editors at top magazines, earn guest posting opportunities and build brands through guest blogging and SEO campaigns, I started thinking, "Why not me?" I began writing and guest blogging and became a columnist for top publications. I encourage you to start somewhere. Maybe you start blogging or guest posting. Maybe you launch a home-based business startup. Just test your crazy ideas in the real world.

That idea, I'm sure, wouldn't have popped in my head if I had zero digital marketing experience. As soon as the idea developed, I visualized the whole venture, reviewed it and got to work.

Starting your own online magazine isn't rocket science. There's no magic trick. All you need is a simple smart plan supported by action, patience and hard work. Show up today. Your readers are hungry for more!

AUTHOR BIOGRAPHY

Dillon Kivo is an American serial entrepreneur, author and keynote speaker. Kivo is the Founder and Editor-in-Chief at Kivo Daily, a business and entrepreneurship magazine that offers a daily dose of business advice for digital startup founders.

Kivo has been named by HuffPost as one of the top personal branding experts. Kivo's work has been featured in Forbes, Inc., Entrepreneur, MSNBC and other top-tier publications as a thought leader in the media industry. He advises some of the most iconic Fortune 500 companies, celebrities, nonprofits and executives around the world. He has spoken about entrepreneurship, branding and public relations to audiences at several universities around the U.S.

Where to Find Dillon
www.kivodaily.com

*"Partner with professional freelancers
and content creators."*

Great Content Needs a Great Writer, a Purpose, and the Right Approach

By Issac Thomas

Getting premium content for your business is no easy deal. Many businesses fail in their marketing strategies because they lack content that distinguishes them as a brand. Creating good content depends on three aspects:

- The Approach
- The Vision
- The Writer

I will talk about all three aspects based on my personal experiences and what I have learned in the past few years working in the Industry.

"Have a 360-degree Approach, Buddy."

This is what my CEO said to me yesterday.

I was struggling for the past few days. I was at the helm of four marketing projects all in different niches. Things were spiraling out of control. There was too much content to be created. They were to be scheduled at specific times and they all needed to be in sync with a theme and a content bucket. I was working around the clock, but the output wasn't great, just satisfactory. When you know you can give your best, better seems underwhelming. I knew there was a problem and had no idea what it was and how to cope with it.

As usual, I went to my CEO because he mentors me well and has a vast pool of experience to back what he says. I told him what I was going through and he resonated with my thoughts. He wanted to talk to me about my dipping form. He agreed there was too much work on my plate, he said, "I can do that with ease if I properly think through it." He continued, "Issac, one of my problems is you have become a doer. If I wanted someone to write content and push through deadlines, I can hire freelancers from Upwork, it isn't a difficult task for me. You are a guy with indefinite potential and just being a doer doesn't suit you. Come out of your limitation and start strategizing what you are doing. You need to see through your work, organize it and plan the whole day before you enter your office."

It takes just 15 minutes to plan, see through your whole day, decide the amount of time you must give to every brand and stick to it. If currently, you are working on four brands, give all of them two hours each. Do not mix all of them because that would create a confusing mess and take a lot of your time.

> *When you are writing a blog, have an outline ready, so that you never waste time organizing your thoughts and thinking what to write. Always strive to keep your mind clear and clutter-less that way you will have clear direction and you can work faster.*

He continued, "Google Earth is one of the best tools I have ever used."

I asked why? He said, "Because Google Earth gives me a 360-degree view to all the places I wish to see. Have a 360-degree approach to work," he said, "look through all possibilities, think of the worst scenarios and be prepared."

"Come out of your limitation and start strategizing what you are doing. You need to see through your work, organize it and plan the whole day before you enter your office." #TheGrowthHackingBook #GrowthHackingMovement #GrowthHackingDay

If You Are Running a Startup, Have a Long-Term Vision

I have worked with a lot of startups as a freelancer. In this digital era, there are a lot of young entrepreneurs who are donning the hats of CEOs and Co-founders. Many aspire to start their venture someday and become a part of the big growing startup community. I am a firm believer that startups in coming days will be the antidote to a job crisis in our country. As a writer, after having worked with many CEO's and co-founders, I see one glaring error in the whole working process of a startup. I am not saying everyone, but most startups don't have a long-term vision or a universal theme.

Most of them would discuss how to get more leads. How do we get more engagement on our posts? Oh! Write and post anything from the latest trends? It is about daily posting something or other across different social media channels and just doing it for the sake of doing it. The whole social media and content marketing revolves around weekly impressions and profile visits.

Week after week, there would be pressure on writers on what to do next. Getting new ideas, each day, week after week makes it difficult for writers who in turn become restless, then rather than flexing their creative muscles, they take the easy way and go with what is trending.

You are creating content that everyone else is creating too, making the whole marketing process mundane and ineffective. Without a unique brand voice, how will a startup or a new business stand apart from the crowd? When your content looks the same as thousand of others in the market, you are part of the crowd. When you are part of the crowd, how will your audience recognize you?

This is what most startups face and because they do not find their unique brand voice, their whole digital marketing strategy falls flat in a few months. Now, as a CEO or Founder of a startup, if you are reading this, go through the Ted Talk, given by Simon Sinek on: ***How do great leaders inspire action?***

As per Simon, most organizations know what they are doing, many of them know how they are doing it, but very few organizations know why they are doing what they are doing. By why, it doesn't always mean making a profit or the results. Why means: What is the purpose of your organization? What are your beliefs? Why do you exist?

People buy from you not for what you do but for why you do it. Figure out the why of your organization and figure out why you are doing what you are doing and build a vision around it. Create a universal theme and make different content buckets around it.

Two days ago, I was giving a session on ***"Personal branding through social media"*** in Delhi. During the session, a girl named Gurpreet asked me, how can she grow her mother's Instagram profile organically without going for unethical hacks like follow for follow?

I asked her, what kind of content does she post? She said her mother is into knitting. They post pictures and videos about knitting. I asked, why do you do that? So you can sell more sweaters?

She said, no. Her mother wants to teach knitting for free and wants to spread awareness about it.

I said, so do a few changes in your profile. Write your Instagram bio as:

Using knitting as a medium to empower women and make them self-dependent with the hashtags #empoweringwomen #fashion #women

This makes you seem in sync and pursuit of a bigger vision. Here, empowering women through knitting is your vision and a long-term mission you want to pursue. That way, it gives you a window to connect with a broader audience with a higher purpose.

I asked her to follow a few hashtags on Instagram like *fashion, knitting, clothes, women empowerment and skills.* Once she followed these hashtags, I asked her to like and comment on the top five posts of those hashtags, which will get more visibility to her profile. Here fashion, knitting, clothes, women empowerment, and skills are the content buckets that can be formed from the universal theme.

When you know what your vision and your bigger universal theme are, it becomes easier to form content buckets out of them. When you have the content buckets ready, you know what kind of topics you need to create content. That gives you a clear idea on what to develop. Once you become consistent with the type of content you create; you will develop your brand voice, and that will surely create an impact.

Your vision — Using knitting as a medium to empower women and make them self-dependent is a tree and the content buckets like fashion and women empowerment are your branches. When you water this tree with better content and add fertilizer in the form of ideas, it will give you fruits in the form of long-term engagement and a dedicated fan base who love what you do and why you do it.

Keep your Writers for a Longer Term

Yes, hire writers for a long term. When you hire a team of writers, hire carefully with long-term goals in mind. Put in extra effort to understand if they will sync with the culture of your company. Once you hire them, give them time to settle down. Let them know what your company is all about and start giving them work slowly. Let them grasp your long-term vision and the kind of content they need to create.

If you ask me why should writers be hired for a longer term? The reason is simple. The more a writer gets familiar with you and your company, the better content he or she can churn out for you. It is all about consistency and longevity. The more two professionals work together, the better their chemistry becomes with time. So, with time once they know you and understand you, they will delve deeper to create even better content, they will come up with new ideas, and better strategies as well. After all, experience counts, and as an organization, hiring and firing are only going to hurt your long-term prospects because everything takes time, money and other resources. Use your money carefully and treat a writer as a long-term resource. Give your writer the best salary and perks as per industry standards because if you want the best content to build a brand, you need to give the best to your writer.

> *A writer is the most critical aspect to creating great content. If you treat them well, not only will they bring a 360-degree approach to their work, they will bring your vision to life. As a brand, you will resonate across the whole digital realm.*

Special Note: This chapter would be incomplete if I don't share a LinkedIn post, that was widely loved by the writer's community. Have a read. It is for everyone who wants to start a career in content writing.

How to Become a Great Writer?

If you are fresher and wish to get into content writing, I would suggest you do three things:

1. Start a blog
2. Write on platforms like Medium and Quora
3. Create an Instagram handle and Facebook page

Show your expertise and pile up some views, likes and comments. Learn the basic three strategies:

- Google analytics
- Content marketing
- Inbound marketing

Read some good articles on writing hacks, social media hacks and how you can improve your online presence. Apply them on your social media accounts, keep experimenting and trying. Have fun as you learn!

Stay longer on these two websites:

- Content marketing institute
- Copyblogger

Follow some good writers, consume good content, read good books, understand the language and improve your vocabulary.

Once you do all the above for a month, check LinkedIn, and other job searching sites for some good job offers and apply.

Also, research and check out the startups in your city, see if they are into marketing and need a writer to create content for them. If they do, meet them and say, you would be glad to join their team.

AUTHOR BIOGRAPHY

Issac Thomas is a digital marketer by profession, and a writer by heart. He started his career as a content writer and is currently working as the Deputy Manager at Markivis, a year old marketing firm that is slowly but steadily gaining a foothold on the B2B marketing landscape. As a marketer, he loves experimenting and testing different marketing methodologies to get the best results for his clients and company. During his free time, he loves reading books and scribbling poetry on Instagram.

Where to Find Isaac
www.markivis.com

"People buy from you not for what you do but for why you do it. Figure out the why of your organization and figure out why you are doing what you are doing and build a vision around it."

Building Marketing Assets That Appreciate In Value While Generating a Modest Income for Many Years to Come

By Dennis Langlais

—◇—

What has convinced many to implement the information I am about to share is the following example.

As our population grows, more and more towns form and some become well established cities. It seems like many of these rural towns start with a gas station. As time passes more and more people pass by and eventually that gas station becomes the center of town. More and more traffic, more and more sales, and the land value persistently rises.

Building a web presence delivers in the same fashion. A business owner invests time and effort into creating a functional website that handles more and more of the daily work, like online purchases, online help, instructions, customer management and so much more.

Best of all is working your way up the rankings in the search engines like Google where you acquire "street corner" visibility, just as a gas station enjoys. It's pretty hard for anyone to come in and take your pole position, because everyone one wants the quick fix. In the past six years there has been a popular website breed coming to the forefront called a funnel. A funnel is a landing page (one page website) that has very narrow and specific information to encourage visitors to give up their email address. An autoresponder then sends them a series of emails to take them through a very strategic sales process. This is an effective model, however it takes highly skilled copywriters to create this version of a website. I also should point out that this model requires you to use methods of paid advertising like Google Adwords and Facebook Ad campaigns.

What if I was to share with you how taking this approach and investing time and money into building your website to produce income in the short term, and to prepare it so that if and when you decide to sell your company, the website becomes the biggest asset you have? Sound good?

Lets Start Growth Hacking

Growth Hack #1

Understand the simple principles of SEO (search engine optimization), which optimizes your website so that you provide information that your prospective clients would love to get their hands on.

Become a master of answering questions, providing information for their betterment, and giving away all your secrets. Focus on writing all of this in such a way that a computer understands not a human, by using accurate, exact and descriptive language.

Most of us know that D.O.J. means Department of Justice. I encourage you not to assume that your reader or the search engines know what you're talking about. It's something that can take some getting used to but many businesses have their own jargon that some may understand and some will not. No readers should have to guess.

The basics of content creation are super simple and anyone who makes time to curate it, can do it. You may find your webpage ranking within just a few days by following these simple techniques:

"I encourage you not to assume that your reader or the search engines know what you're talking about." #TheGrowthHackingBook #GrowthHackingMovement #GrowthHackingDay

Title - The tile can be the same as your heading or in "HTML" its called H1 the tag form is <h1> for header. Let's say you want to rank for "Best Coffee In San Diego," the heading and title should include those exact words.

Sub Heading - this is an elaboration of your heading and also can double as your page description. The page description first appears on the page within the 'meta tags' they are not visible unless you do the following:

- Google Chrome: Go to: View > Developer > View Source.
- Safari: Enable Developer in Preferences at the bottom under Advanced. Once you have checked the box, go to the Developer tab > show Web Inspector and you will be able to examine the code.

This is basically what search engines see. There are rumors that they have technology to visually scan your page but it's not proven as a priority.

Images: images are becoming a more and more valuable way to market your company. As they are added to a web page you can name the actual image based on your keyword search "Best Coffee In San Diego" that may look something like this, 'Best_Coffee_In_San_Diego.jpg'. Along with this you can add Image Title & Alt tags. It's encouraged to use the relevant keywords there as well.

Go take a look for yourself. Search Google for a keyword phrase of interest and click on the images tab. While you are at it, try the Videos tab (more on that later).

Paragraphs: We have included the keywords in our Heading and Sub Heading and they don't have to be in order, however I encourage it if possible.

Next is your Paragraphs, Bullets, Bolded text. The obvious is to have relative content in a paragraph form with your keyword phrase included. If you can reuse the words in your phrases at least 4 to 5 times throughout your page you are doing well.

These simple considerations will do wonders to start you on the path to getting ranked in search engines. Please take note that some industries are much more aggressive in their ranking strategies. In this case we encourage you to go after what we call the low hanging fruit keyword phrases. Phrases that are not so mainstream but will at least help you catch some of the traffic. Each industry has its main go to searches however there are less important ones that you can work towards ranking for.

Once you have obtained a high rank for any keyword it's likely that you will strong hold that position give or take a few spots for a long time. I began using this strategy back in 2006 and created many pages that got ranked in the top 10 for words that were popular searches in my industry and today in 2019, even after I sold that company in 2013, and the purchaser has not done any sort of improvement, those pages still rank well. That is what we call a long-term investment or appreciating asset. When determining the value of the company the website presence was a key factor. Rightfully so, as we see many years later those pages are generating income all while maintaining a decent rank.

Since then, I have created a competing company and have implemented many newer ranking strategies and eventually because I am continually using newer strategies, I will surpass that company in search engine rankings.

Videos: I highly encourage you to create videos of content and questions where you can. There is no need to hire a video team; all of this can be done on a smart phone. Every phone can capture very high quality video and directly upload the videos straight to Youtube.

Similar to your webpage content use the same principles I shared with content, by having a Header, Title and Paragraphs that use the keywords, then link that video to the pages you have created which have the same keywords. **The link is a must!** I also encourage you to embed these videos on your pages too.

Questions: If you type a question in the search bar on Google you will notice as of recent, they now have the ability to scan webpages and pull out great answers. This is awesome right? If you master the art of creating questions and answers this is a great new way to rank in Google and build creditability. They are called "snippets" in these snippets Google will include a link to your page so that the users can go to your page for more information. As I mentioned earlier the more you are descriptive and make the most complete answers, understanding not to assume anything is understood and be clear, you can soon enough find yourself landing some prime real estate in the Google ranks. This is one I am taking very seriously because I believe the credibility part will serve you well.

Definitions: Although I do not have any proof that creating definitions of keywords or phrases in your industry will make you more money, I cannot see how it will hurt you. I know personally I am constantly trying to define and understand words, why not have them all conveniently available for your visitors, just like a gas station conveniently has gum, soda and coffee right there while you are paying. It makes complete sense right?

Last Hack That Just May Transform Your Business and Return Profits You Never Expected

I really think you are going to like this one, so be ready. What if right now you and I could find new business for you, utilizing assets you already have, that are not being used? Would that make all of this reading worth it?

Let's begin...

1. Make a list of 5 search terms you would love to rank for in Google.

2. Take the first one... I will use "Podcasting" since I have a podcast and it needs to generate more income. Read carefully because this is a gold mine: As you type the words into the search query notice the words that start to populate for you.

Some of you maybe looked at this as a complete pain before, but what Google is showing you is what 'others,' possibly your prospective clients, 'ARE TYPING' Google is not guessing, they are giving you actual search queries. These are the popular searches related to the words you type in the search bar.

What I see for podcasting is a list: podcasting 101, podcasting microphone, podcasting equipment, podcasting software. The question we have to ask our selves is WHY NOT create service, products or information about any or all of these search terms to gain traffic even if some of them are not so favorable to your offering, they will serve you well in gaining traffic. We see all the time companies create a product that complements what they offer. Pepsi bought Fritos chips because well, when you drink soft drinks, you just may want some chips. If I am a famous podcaster, why not have my own signature microphone. I do not have to actually create my own but I may be able to work with a company to create a signature series version and make extra cash.

In one of my old companies, I ran a BMX stunt show that performed shows across the US. We had a variety of expensive ramp setups and the bigger more expensive ones sat in storage 280 days a year. By doing this same exercise I noticed the keyword phrase "half pipe ramp rental." I went on to make a page with nothing to lose and to my surprise we would get calls from corporations and Hollywood companies to rent the ramps at extremely high prices, more than we sell our BMX show it's self for.

In two years this became 20% of our sales and did not require any riders, or other coordination. We had to just drive to the location and set the ramps up and many times they were just background props. Ask yourself: What assets do you have that can be making you profits? You invested in them for your business, maybe they can be utilized to generate income in other ways for you and increase your profits.

Closing

Today I rely on SEO for all my businesses. I am not excited about using social media. I tried for years and it's just not my thing. I do like ranking in Google using SEO, its simple and anyone who can type can use it.

This led me to create a software platform where anyone who wants to focus on Google-izing their web presence can create websites with ease. By adding the suggested content, the software creates the webpages for you, there are no design skills needed.

Website Building Software That Helps Your Business Get 'Google-ized'

www.rankingmastery.com's proprietary software generates 100s of landing pages utilizing the top keywords, that customers search with in your industry.

Establishing your business in the ranks of Google is an investment that will yield results indefinitely, where paying for rankings is only good as long as you keep paying.

I invested time in ranking one of my companies back in 2008. My rankings played a big part in the valuation when it came time to sell it. It's been over 10 years, and no changes to the content since the sale and it still ranks competitively. That's an appreciating asset. I like to relate this accomplishment to establishing a gas station in a new town, you own the street corner and that corner, as the town grows around you gains value and it's much harder to be knocked off the block.

Ranking Mastery is a website builder that helps YOU Google-ize your website, with no design skills needed. Just create your content and send us your photos and we edit and size them for you.

Simple to Use and Here's How it Works

1. Choose the keyword phrases you want to be found on Google.

2. Add them to our proprietary SEO Association Tool.

3. Associate keywords in logical phrases.

4. Add your content relevant to these areas, we suggest: About, Mission, Expect & Why.

5. Add to your libraries, any testimonials, videos, social media, questions, podcasts and team members.

6. Choose what sections you want to appear on your page.

7. Choose the webpages font theme.

8. Let our tools do the work and you will have hundreds or thousands of landing pages that will begin to be indexed in Google.

Features

- Keyword association to all your content, photos, videos, blogs and events.

- Top rated blog building software.

- Top rated event building software that can do multi-day events.

- Create libraries of your social media, videos, testimonials, team members, questions, podcasts and more.

- Simple to use lead management CRM.

- Automatically builds pages for mobile.

- Access to a variety of professionally designed layouts.

The Best SEO Website Software

- It Works! Nothing compares when it comes to keyword association. All of the competition keywords have to be added to each page manually on all the areas including headlines, content, images, videos, meta tags and titles. This can take hours if done manually, with the website builder, it takes seconds.

- Our website builder helps you focus on content while we focus on design. Each design is created to allow you to add all the essentials a page needs to convert sales as well as rank in search engines.

- When it comes to editing website landing pages for SEO you will find that all your pages will have consistent content, for example: buttons, social media, testimonials, Q/A, phone numbers and addresses. Our platform provides you with a way to change all of that in one place, then updates your pages whether you have 50 or 50,000.

This SEO Website Builder is For You If:

- You are making it a priority once and for all to get ranked in Google searches.

- You do not have website design skills.

- You would rather focus on writing content.

- You would love a website builder that updates all your consistent content at once.

- You want your website automatically designed for mobile phones.

- You want a platform that includes blogging software.

- You want a platform that includes a way to promote your events.

Author Biography

Dennis was born and raised in New England and later moved to San Diego, CA as a successful Professional athlete in the extreme sports world. Always intrigued by marketing Dennis learned many aspects of design, websites and SEO to grow all his business adventures. Some of his wins in business are Perfection on Wheels BMX Stunt Team, Appprocessor, Codie Dog Interactive, FIVE Minute Bark Podcast. Pro athlete to business owner to web marketer, to podcasting, to programming Dennis love the adventure of learning.

Rankingmastery.com was created in 2019 by accident.. YES! What in the moment seemed to be a disastrous situation turned into a revolutionary idea. Time and time again life leads us down paths that we don't really understand, but when we embrace it vs defer from it something spectacular can come our way. rankingmastery.com has developed into the answer that Dennis struggled with when creating visibility on the web by building webpages that rank with SEO.

"Establishing your business in the ranks of Google is an investment that will yield results indefinitely, where paying for rankings is only good as long as you keep paying."

Essential SEO Growth Hacks – Learn to Rank your Site Faster

By Surabh Tiwari

Staying ahead of the competition and succeeding in business on the Internet today can be quite difficult. An effective online presence will help your business reach out to new customers and clients and improve all aspects of your business, taking it to greater heights.

There are many marketing strategies that can help you promote your products and services, for example: Facebook advertising, Instagram marketing and Google Adwords.

If you want to grow your business organically, this is where Search Engine Optimization (SEO) continues to play a pivotal role in making sure that you're visible to the public. Independent business owners need to double down on SEO if they want to stay ahead of their competitors and grow their audience.

Getting started with SEO can be difficult at first and takes time, however once your site is ranked and appears in search engines, it helps to generate organic traffic to your website, which will also produce leads and sales.

To make it easy for you I am going to talk about the top SEO Growth Hacks, so you can stick with the right methods and strengthen your SEO game.

There are more than 200 Ranking factors, according to Google's secret Algorithm.

As Google AI is getting smarter day by day, social signals, technical SEO, https, On-Page SEO, Voice Search, Website UX, Mobile first indexing, Page Speed is becoming dominant.

"Getting started with SEO can be difficult at first and takes time, however once your site is ranked and appears in search engines, it helps to generate organic traffic to your website, which will also produce leads and sales." #TheGrowthHackingBook #GrowthHackingMovement #GrowthHackingDay

SEO Growth Hacks

Tweak your Technical SEO and on-page SEO

Page Speed

One of the most important parts of Technical SEO is page speed. Google now considers page speed as one of its main ranking factors. If a website takes more than seven seconds to load, the user is more likely to skip your website and move on to something else, so it is extremely important for you to look after your website's loading speed.

You can check the loading speed of your website/Blog using tools like **PageSpeed Insights and GTMetrix.**

Responsive Design

Responsive Design refers to the responsiveness of your website to the screen that is accessing it. A website must adjust from small phone screens to large desktop screens.

When viewing your website through a mobile device, a responsive website will shrink down and realign images and text to offer a mobile view. On the other hand for a large desktop screen you will see the full website design.

To determine if your website is mobile friendly or not, take Google's Mobile-Friendly Test.

Mobile-first indexing

Until now, Google has always indexed the desktop version of websites to determine how to rank content. That's all changing. In 2016, Google announced they had plans to shift their algorithm to crawl the mobile versions of sites first.

How To Make Sure Your Site Is Ready For Mobile-First Indexing

Use a Mobile-Friendly Design (You can test your site using Google's free Mobile-Friendly Test tool).

Make sure your website content is similar on both desktop and mobile versions.

You need to ensure that your site loads fast in the mobile version.

Some Other Essential On-Page SEO Factors You Need to Know

- Image Optimization
- Page titles and meta descriptions
- Structured Data and Schema Markup
- HTTPS / SSL
- Verify Your Website/blog in Search Console
- Add Google Analytics to the Site and Set KPI and goal.

- Check the Robots.txt file
- XML Sitemap
- Site and URL Structure and Permalinks

Competitor Research to find SEO opportunities where competitors are lacking

The most important part of SEO is Competitor Research.

You will never be able to apply the perfect SEO hacks to your website unless you know what your competitors are doing. By doing competitor research, we simply figure out what tactics our competitors are applying, what kind of back-links they have, and what kind of keywords they are targeting, then we use that information to create an informed and targeted SEO strategy.

Doing competitor research is not as hard as it seems, as there are quite a lot of tools to help you. However, among all the tools, Ahrefs and SEMrush are the most popular SEO tools available and using both of these tools is super easy.

Let me share a guide with you:

Step 1: First of all, go to Ahrefs or SEMrush. Both of these tools are paid, so you will have to get a subscription at first before you start using them.

Step 2: Simply enter your competitor's domain or let the tool identify your organic competitors.

Step 3: The tool will look for details about the competitor and come up with data on competitor's search rankings, the keywords they are targeting, number of backlinks, number of referring domains and more.

Creating In-depth Content

Content is 'King,' and you cannot deny this fact; however, there is quite a lot of content out there that lacks quality. Here are some tips, which will help you to create in-depth content that attracts the right leads to your business.

Start With Keyword Research

One of the first steps to creating in-depth content is doing proper keyword research. If you have identified keywords, which are easy to rank for, then you will be able to improve the number of leads to your business without doing too much hard work. For keyword research, both SEMrush and Ahrefs have good keyword research tools in their toolkits.

Start With A Great Introduction

Now that you have found a great keyword to work with, start writing the article by coming up with a great introduction.

The Introduction to any content is extremely important. If your introduction does not connect with the user and has them wanting to read more about what you are discussing, the user will quickly leave your website. Write a great introduction, which hooks the visitor.

Understand the concept of user intent and choose topics accordingly, by targeting long tail versions of your main keywords.

Summarize the topic in the first two to three paragraphs. People are looking for solutions to their problems, so as directly as possible, in the first few paragraphs you must offer them a solution. This will help to catch their attention and compel them to read further.

Research and Write

The main part is writing the in-depth content that explains everything about a topic. You must research your topic well and then form your article. Check your top 10 ranked websites and look over their content. Create a structure for your content that is even better.

E-A-T Content

You will need to focus on E-A-T Content. E-A-T stands for expertise, authoritativeness and trustworthiness.

E-A-T is one of the metrics used by Google's evaluators to rank pages. The simple logic behind the metric is that high quality pages pass a high level of EAT when the low quality pages don't. This means that you need to focus on creating high quality content.

The question is, how do you master E-A-T?

Your content must be enough to satisfy the needs of the user. For example, if they are searching for how to fix a problem, then your content must help them solve this problem. Now they won't have to look for the solution on other websites.

Your website must have a positive reputation for its page topics.

Your website must feature all the auxiliary information like 'About us,' 'Contact,' and 'Customer Service.'

Your website must feature supplementary content, which enhances the user's experience on the web page.

The webpage should be maintained, edited and updated from time to time.

Content Formatting

Proper content formatting is critical. Writing content is half and formatting the content is the other half. Whenever you are posting a new article on your website, make sure to use correct content formatting.

Your content must have proper headlines (use Header tags like h1, h2, h3, etc.).

Make the content scan-able by bolding the main keywords and important parts. Break the content into small paragraphs, so the user can scroll down and scan your content easily.

Some Other Things Keep In Mind

- Write a compelling headline with main keyword, power words, emotions and brackets. A good title will encourage users to click on your article from SERP.

- Interlink your blog posts so that search engines can crawl your site easily. It also reduces your bounce rate.
- Use bullet points.
- Use Table of Contents.
- Use Appealing Graphics, Memes, Infographics and Videos.
- Link out to reputable, trusted resources to prove to Google your site sits in a trusted, authority neighborhood.

Backlink Building

Without backlinks, it is quite tough to rank your website well. You will need to have a proper backlink building strategy for your website. There are quite a lot of strategies that you can follow to build backlinks for your website. For example, you can do a guest post on other websites and link your website using backlinks.

You can find a broken link on a website and ask that blog owner if they can replace the link with your website's link and so on.

Some of the best link building tactics are: infographic submission, business citation sites, skyscraper and HARO technique.

Maintain backlinks by performing bookkeeping to see if the links you have made are still live or not.

AUTHOR BIOGRAPHY

Saurabh is a Digital Marketer with many years experience working with reputed SEO companies, and has helped many clients get ranked on the top searches of Google. Saurabh founded his own SEO company AllDigiTrends. He is also the lead author of his popular Indian blog TechiBhai.

Where to Find Saurabh
www.twitter.com/krsaurabht
www.linkedin.com/in/saurabhtiwari2
www.alldigitrends.net
techibhai.com

"Until now, Google has always indexed the desktop version of websites to determine how to rank content. That's all changing. In 2016, Google announced they had plans to shift their algorithm to crawl the mobile versions of sites first."

GRABBING MEDIA ATTENTION TO GROW YOUR PERSONAL BRAND

By Deepak V. Maddila

Understanding how people behave and getting them to feel a certain way and take a particular action is how I look at Public Relations as a whole. These people are reporters and journalists, your customers, your internal team, stakeholders and anyone else you want to influence.

Personal Branding is the process of establishing an image for your target audience.

In this chapter, I'm going to talk about social media hacks that help will encourage reporters and journalists to reach out to you for an interview or a feature. I'll also show you how to fine-tune your social media profiles so that journalists perceive you as an expert in your niche.

Get the Press to Approach You and Not the Other Way Around

I'm going to help you grab the attention of reporters using social media, primarily Facebook advertising, even on a minimal budget.

It can be straightforward when it comes to getting press. If you're an expert in your industry, you'll need to prove your expertise to the media outlets, who would want to feature you. Once they see you're an expert in your field, and your niche is something they regularly cover, they'll want to reach out to interview you. When they see posts or ads on Facebook that shows your expertise and the big name clients you've worked with or interviewed, they'll understand that you're great at what you do.

To implement this hack, you'll need a beginner level understanding of Facebook Ads and how to set them up. It would be best if you were a content creator or someone ready to create content. You'll also need a "Public Figure" Facebook Page that's connected to your "Public Figure" Instagram Page.

Why Facebook Ads?

Facebook has advertising options parallel to none. Users are served Facebook Ads based on our interests, behaviors and the demographics we belong to. Facebook has collected data for many years and created the most powerful advertising tool available. Legend says Facebook knows us better than our spouse. Again, the purpose of this hack is to get a reporter or a media outlet to reach out to you.

Here's the Step-by-Step Process

First, perform research to find which niche your story or message fits with and make a list of the media outlets you want to target. We'll use Facebook ads to target people who work in specific media outlets.

After opening 'Ads Manager,' click to the main menu on the top left. Click on 'Assets,' then click 'Audiences' (see images below).

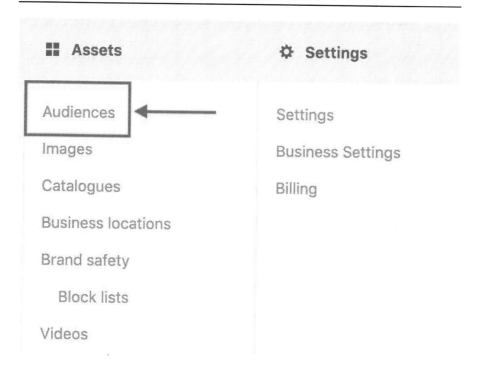

A new page will open, click on 'Create Audience,' then click 'Saved Audience.'

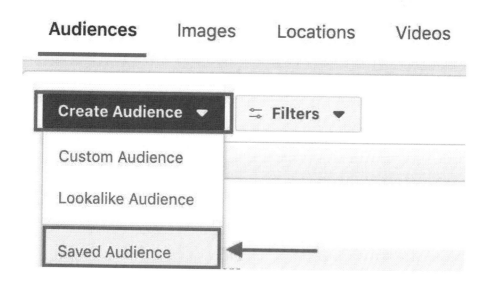

In 'Create a Saved Audience' box, name your audience based on the niche or region, example: India, United States, etc. Find the 'Detailed Targeting' menu under options: Age, Gender and Languages.

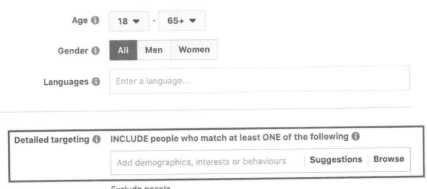

Click 'Browse' in the 'Detailed Targeting' menu and unlock the vast array of options that Facebook Ads offer.

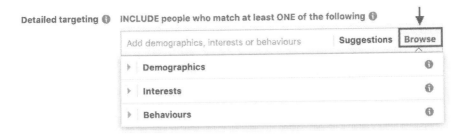

When you click 'Demographics,' you'll see options like Education, Financial, Life Events, Parents, Relationships and Work. These options show the vast amount of data Facebook has collected about us. From our work backgrounds to our relationship status, Facebook knows almost everything.

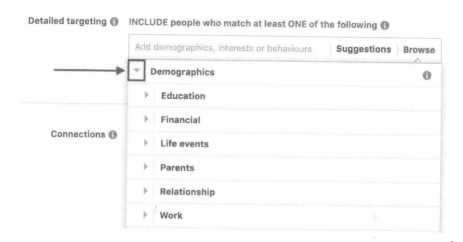

Choose the 'Work' option and click 'Employers.'

A search bar will open asking you to search for employers. Here you will use the Media list that you prepared earlier. Type the names of the media outlets and choose them as shown below. After selecting the ones you want, click 'Create Audience' and you will have successfully created and saved an audience full of media personnel. At the end of this explanation, I've provided lists of media outlets in India and the United States.

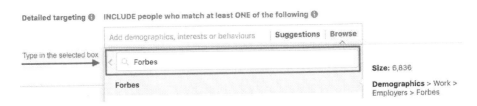

Your next step is to create posts that builds your authority. Your aim is to attract the reporters' attention, first think about your content from a reporter's perspective.

What kind of posts will grab their attention and compel them to reach out to you? These posts can be about a major influencer who vouches for you, summarizing your previous press features, an interview you have done with an industry leader, a short one-minute video message that gels with current newsworthy trends.

When it comes to length, short, one-minute videos work best. Humans have short attention spans, which is why Snapchat and Instagram stories are a huge hit. When creating your video, use the first three seconds to hook the viewer, 3-15 seconds to communicate the problem and opportunity, and during the last ten-seconds encourage them to take action with a 'call to action'.

Choose four posts that perform well with your organic reach and click on 'Boost Post' at the bottom right of every post on your Facebook Page.

When the boost post box opens, choose the objective of your post, either send them to your Website or the Contact or Media/Press page. Choose your 'Saved Audience' and set your budget at $1.00 or Rs. 70, then click the 'Boost' button and the ad will go live within a few minutes.

Choosing a minimal budget is what makes this hack so effective. It gives you exposure to the elite media houses on a limited budget. My mentor, Dennis Yu, CEO of Blitzmetrics, named this: 'Dollar-a-Day Strategy'.

The great thing about this hack is that it works with all social media channels, even LinkedIn. When it comes to LinkedIn, you can use a similar strategy via paid ads or you can gain from the enormous organic traction that LinkedIn is having right now. Add reporters and journalists to your connections and create compelling posts to grab their attention.

"Understanding behavior, getting people to feel a particular way and take a specific action is Public Relations." #PublicRelations #TheGrowthHackingBook #GrowthHackingMovement #GrowthHackingDay

Important media outlets found in the Employer section of the Facebook Ads tool:

Indian Media Houses

- The Times of India
- Aaj Tak
- The Hindu
- The Economic Times
- Financial Times
- Hindustan Times
- The Indian Express
- Times Now
- NDTV
- Zee News
- Dainik Bhaskar
- Dainik Jagran
- India Today
- Deccan Chronicle
- ABP News
- India TV

US Media Houses

- The Guardian
- Ellen DeGeneres
- People Magazine
- SFGate
- Time Warner Cable
- TIME
- The Late Show With Stephen Colbert
- Chron.com from the Houston Chronicle
- NBC Nightly News With Lester Holt
- Today Show
- CBS News
- The San Diego Union-Tribune
- Live with Regis and Kelly
- USA TODAY
- iHeartMedia Inc.
- Detroit Free Press
- The New York Post
- Weekly World News
- The Late Late Show with James Corden
- Fox News
- CBS Radio
- Jimmy Kimmel
- The Buffalo News
- Dr Oz Show
- Business Insider
- Mashable
- CNN
- Newsweek
- The Dallas Morning News
- Newsday
- The Sacramento Bee
- New York Times
- MSNBC
- Miami Herald
- The Seattle Times
- The Boston Globe
- Las Vegas Review-Journal
- Washington Post
- Chicago Tribune
- Los Angeles Times
- CNET
- NBC
- The Oprah Magazine

By using this strategy, you will position yourself as an authority figure in the eys of the media. When they visit your profile page, they will see you as an expert, providing you have created it in a way that positions you as an expert.

Fine Tune Your Social Media Profiles:

Social Media Profile: Your profile has to communicate your personality as well as showcase your industry authority.

Headshot: A professional headshot image communicates your confidence. It creates a feeling of trust and helps people believe in you when they visit your profile. Avoid pictures where you are far in the background and can't be seen. Your face should occupy 60% of the image. A good headshot profile picture is an excellent way to display your professionalism.

Achievements Over Titles in Your Biography: After seeing your profile picture, reporters and other people view your biography. Reporters value achievements and accomplishments over titles. Some people have a terrible habit of showcasing their roles and leaving it there. Instead, mention your achievements first and write about your title and role later.

First Three Posts: After going through your bio, if they are still interested, they will view your posts. Your first three posts are vital so make sure you are talking about your industry and any recent achievements of yours, with wins first. Remove temporary updates or posts from your profile. A significant achievement may compel them to engage with your post. Later, you can direct message them and start a conversation.

I hope these strategies help you in growing your business and gaining more press coverage. Social Media is where a lot of consumers spend their time, which makes it a great tool for getting the attention of the media. News updates, including breaking news, is now first shared on social media and reporters are connecting with various experts online through social media to learn more about them and the products and services they offer. Leveraging social media to share your message can attract many new opportunities for your business, grow your brand and help get you featured by the press.

Author Biography

Deepak V. Maddila is the Founder and CEO of DVM Media, PR Agency. He's a PR/Marketing Strategist and a TEDx Speaker. He has worked with influencers who have millions of followers and helped them get featured in major publications. Inc. Magazine has named him a Marketing Expert and he's listed as one of 2018s 30 Game Changers in India. Apart from entrepreneurship, Deepak loves physics and is a co-author of a research paper that's been published for an IEEE International Conference.

Where to Find Deepak
www.linkedin.com/in/deepakvmaddila
www.dvmmedia.co

"Reporters value achievements and accomplishments over titles. People have a terrible habit of showcasing their roles and leaving it there. Instead, mention your achievements first and write about your tribe or role later."

How To Pitch Journalists For Public Relations Success

By Rahul Singh

"Public Relations is a continuous process that starts from the very first day when an idea emerges. An Organization and it's Public Relations can never be divided. Ultimately the people you serve matter the most." - Rahul Singh

After working for years in the media industry I have come to describe Public Relations as communication that deals with the science of the human brain and the art of formulating words that make an impact on the receiver. Public Relations is the bridge that gaps what a business wants to portray and what the public perceives.

It's not easy to portray exactly what you want to pass onto the public and have them understand that you actually care about their problems and queries. It is necessary though, and building relationships with your customers and clients is as important to you and your business, as it is to them.

Good public relations involves sharing your vision and values with all people, your audience as well as people you partner with, who can help and support you.

Journalists work as the link between a business and a media outlet. Public Relations professionals understand both business and media which makes it helpful to rely on your PR manager and the strategies they identify to be important for your business success.

Based on the findings of Harold Lasswell and the '*Magic Bullet Theory of Mass Communication,*' the media helps creates an image among the masses.

The information delivered by media has an influential impact on people, mostly due to the credibility factor. Certain information can work to improve the life of people, by providing them with information that can help them.

"Public Relations is a continuous process that starts from the very first moment your business idea emerges. Business and public relations can never be separated because getting your message out is what matters most." #PublicRelations #PR #Communication #Mediarelation #Mediapitch #TheGrowthHackingBook #GrowthHackingMovement #GrowthHackingDay

I have found people can make mistakes while dealing with journalists; here are tips to help:

Journalists Are Not Easy Nuts to Crack

Journalists are looking for outstanding stories with exclusive information, which they tailor to fit their own writing style and expertise. Invest time in your content. Many journalists prefer to experience a product or service for themselves before writing about them for publication.

Journalists have a huge influence on public opinion due to having the image of being a credible source of information.

Journalists Expect You to Follow Their Work Regularly

Follow the journalist's work, which helps you keep track of their work patterns and their style of writing. It also helps when you personalise messages to a journalist. Do not bother the journalist with trivial questions; rather use your network to gather as much information as you can, then seek their insights for the story.

Attention Seeking Can Be Good

Mass media is the best way to reach out to your audience, however maintaining a great image of your company in front of the media can be a tough task.

More often business organizations consider themselves newsworthy but the question is are they always doing something worthy of grabbing peoples' attention? If not then the focus should be on bringing something new to the table that will help them get into the news.

Having something solid to provide to the media is an undeniable pre-requisite. Make sure whatever the company does is newsworthy, makes sense to the public and acts as an add-on to their knowledge and understanding about the company.

Journalists are already under pressure to get exclusive information for their publications. With journalists receiving so many emails from Public Relations professionals from different organizations, it's critical to have a subject line that stands out from all the other emails they receive.

Online Media Room

Create a page on your website for your Online Media Room. Include any media coverage pieces, company information and any images a journalist may need to help them write a story about your company.

Make it simple for journalists and reporters to quickly access important and relevant information and copy it for use in their own documents.

Include large headlines for each item on your page, to make it quick and easy for journalists to find the information and images they are looking for.

What To Include In Your Online Media Room and Press Kit:

1. Images for Company Logo, Team Members and Main Product Images
2. Company Name, History, Mission and Purpose
3. Company Contact Information and Location with Google Map if relevant
4. Links to Articles, Interviews, prior Media Reports and Press Releases
5. Links to Annual Reports and Company Yearbooks
6. Links to Social Media Business Pages
7. Quotes, Reviews, Testimonials and Awards

Follow Media Outlets, Reporters and Journalists on Social Media

Follow the journalists and their work through social media, don't go overboard and make them wary of you. Find opportunities to have real conversations through their posts and send them greetings for their outstanding stories.

When they do create a story about you and your business, be grateful and show your appreciation.

Most importantly, take the time to meet them in person and build a friendly relationship with them, as well as a professional one.

Keep track of journalists covering similar stories and add them to a database.

Frequently share any changes that occur in your industry.

Developing a friendly relationship and having regular contact with journalists gives you leverage to get your story covered.

Providing journalists with valuable information does work in the long term.

Perfecting Your PR Pitch

Many businesses make mistakes when they pitch their story.

Use all the information you've obtained from your research and put it to good use. Invest some time before you actually reach out to the journalists and decide exactly what you are going to say when you call or meet them in person. This minimizes the chance of slipping in the wrong information at the wrong time.

The pitch mail you send a journalist should be an extension of the summary of information for your organization.

Have your Online Media Room ready to make it easier for reporters and journalists to research your company.

When Your Story Gets Featured, The Game Is Just Starting

Once your story has been featured, use every opportunity to market the media coverage on social media. Regular postings help to instill a good brand image in the public eye.

Share your opinions with people and tag them in the posts. These days social media is the best way to promote your products and services, and your organization. Post and repost.

Tagging people helps to boost the posts' visibility to your target audience. Another benefit of tagging relevant people in the posts is that you can acknowledge their contribution to a specific project, which helps to build a long-term relationship with them.

Using an official page for posts is more effective than posting through your personal social media accounts and serves better audience engagement in the long run.

Getting featured in the media and maintaining great relationships with journalists is part of the Public Relations process. You can never think the ultimate goal of reputation attainment has been reached because just a moment of lag can crumble down the castles you have been building to create a respected brand for your business.

The media plays a great role in helping a business position itself because they understand public psychology. A company that hones its public relation management skills well, will rise up to be leaders in their industry. After all, what matters most is the difference an organization can create for the end users in terms of productivity, information, cognition and more.

One of my friends asked me how I managed to get coverage for my business, and I told her it is: reading and persistence. The more time you spend on reading write-ups from the journalists, to understand their writing styles and patterns, the more it reduces the risk of getting rejected.

There's no shortcut to getting media coverage, the more you relate with members of the media in person, the better your outcomes will be.

There might be thousands of tools that can be used for automated content development and press release distribution, but the impact they create will not be near to when you've met people in person.

AUTHOR BIOGRAPHY

Rahul Singh is the Founder and CEO of PR Agency, *The Publicity Dude*. He's a featured Publicist and Business Columnist. He has helped various corporates and startups to build a solid media presence. He is listed as one of 2018s '30 Game Changers in India' and had been featured in Business magazines like Entrepreneur and Yourstory.

Where to Find Rahul
www.linkedin.com/in/rahulsingh-thepublicitydude
www.thepublicitydude.com

"The more time you spend on reading and research journalists to understand their writing style and interests, the lower the risk of having your pitches rejected."

SOCIAL MEDIA SKILLS

"If you make customers unhappy in the physical world, they might each tell 6 friends. If you make customers unhappy on the Internet, they can each tell 6,000 friends."

JEFF BEZOS

GROWTH HACKING YOUR PRESENCE ON LINKEDIN AND MAKING AN IMPACT

By Yaagneshwaran Ganesh

If you've landed on this chapter, you undoubtedly understand the importance of your LinkedIn profile and the need to make it impactful on your target audience.

First things first: everyone has a unique purpose for using LinkedIn. For some, it can be getting recruited (94% of recruiters use LinkedIn to search for job candidates), building your personal brand, social selling of your products and services and much more. With over 470 million LinkedIn users, how do you stand out and make an impact? This is exactly what I'm going to be sharing with you throughout this chapter.

To set some ground rules: I really respect your time and I won't be discussing very basic information such as the need to have a professional profile picture, a clear headline that defines you, a fully updated profile and recommendations. If you're looking to make an impact with your profile, you've probably already covered these basics. Let's dive into the information and actionable points that will help you growth hack your brand on LinkedIn.

What I've learned in 10 Years on LinkedIn:

The purpose of using LinkedIn has vastly changed over the years from being focused on professional networking to building personal brands.

Though a lot of people want to drive sales conversions from LinkedIn as a channel, you need to realize that LinkedIn is more of a "me channel". People don't want to follow companies, people want to establish their own profiles, connect with other people and promote themselves.

One of the simplest strategies to accomplish this is the transition from LinkedIn's group based engagement to post engagement. The fact that LinkedIn moved away from being primarily desktop focused to mobile focused has contributed to this change as 59% of people access LinkedIn from their smartphones. Instead of getting into groups and waiting for posts to be moderated, more and more people prefer to share their content and post as they go.

Why do People Log onto LinkedIn?

Most of the people who use LinkedIn aren't logging in thinking they're going to solve the challenges inside their companies. Most of them log in for personal reasons, including job searches, checking who viewed their profile, establishing a presence for themselves and so on.

Your message on LinkedIn has no choice but to be focused on people and not companies. Your messaging needs to align with the interests of your target audience so you'll have opportunities to establish meaningful relationships.

Now that we've established the premise, let's discuss how to growth hack your presence on LinkedIn, to be more impactful.

Hacking Your Way to Improving Your Brand Presence

You might've heard a lot of people say, "Produce and share great content". Almost everyone in the content marketing world says this, but is it true?

- It's partly true. Producing quality content consistently and sharing it in a focused environment like LinkedIn offers great potential for you to be perceived as an expert. This is because a good majority of LinkedIn users aren't producers of content; they are consumers of content. The point here is — almost everyone has the ability to produce content. Some produce mediocre content, while others produce brilliant content.

The problem isn't just content production. The actual problem is consumption of content. Do people see your content? If so, do they consume your content and react to it?

To improve your brand presence and to establish yourself as an expert on LinkedIn, you need to make sure that your target audience consumes your content.

Here Are a Few LinkedIn Stats:

- LinkedIn Slideshare alone has 18 million pieces of content.
- There are 9 billion content impressions every week.
- 3 million users share content on LinkedIn on a weekly basis.

Why Are There a Lot of Posts on LinkedIn That Have Zero Engagement? Here Are Some Fundamental Reasons:

- They don't post quality content.
- They aren't consistent.
- More importantly, they don't ask questions.
- They don't explicitly invite their audience for a discussion.
- And in most cases, they haven't clearly identified their target audience.

That's not all. Even if you have done the above things right, there is still a lot of ground to cover.

Cracking the Content Consumption Game on LinkedIn:

One of the most important things to ask yourself when you want to drive content consumption on LinkedIn is, "How long will your post be shown on the content feed," and "What drives that"?

Based on my own personal experiments, I've observed that the engagement of your content in the first hour after you post is super critical. The more people like, share and comment, the longer your posts will stay alive on the feed. What drives engagement? Engagement is solely dependent on the type of content you share and the kind of people that react first.

If you want your posts to be seen by 5,000 people, use this approach:

- Focus on getting five people to react on your post. Make sure those five people have influence over the 5,000 people you are targeting.

- Don't blindly tag those five people, invest in building a relationship with them before involving them on your posts, or you'll end up spamming them.

- Once you get those five people to interact, the target audience you end up reaching will definitely be way north of what you actually targeted.

- Have a group of a few friends from your website who will interact with you as soon as you post your content. This first group is referred to as LinkedIn pods. They're the ones that help give the initial momentum for the visibility of your posts.

Here's Our First Content Experiment

My colleague Manish and I started #coffeeconversations, a video series on LinkedIn about four months ago. It's a series where we discuss various topics in marketing, especially the topics that interest startups. We wanted to reach an audience who were primarily startup marketers and sales professionals.

For the first few posts, we were getting around 300-500 views per post. Then we posted this:

Yaagneshwaran Ganesh

Top 100 Global Martech Influencer | TEDx Speaker | Forbes Council | Auth...

1mo · Edited

#coffeeconversations

Today Manish and I chatted about the people we love to follow to derive inspiration for our marketing. Marketing as such is one field which we need to be constantly updated upon and the learning cycle can never stop.

We shared some of the people whose content we really love, like - Scott Brinker, Tim Soulo, Tom Fishburne, Kotryna Kurt, Dave Trott, Mark Metry, Hala Taha and more.

Feel free to share the ones you follow and what they share about. Let's make this a super repository of the best in business in marketing.

#marketing #branding #content #contentmarketing #martech #customerserv

197 Likes · 49 Comments · 10,764 Views

 Like   Comment   Share

▷ 10,764 views of your video

You can see that this post literally had 49 comments, close to 200 likes and a whopping 10,797 people watching the video, all this within 24 hours.

What actually happened was that I tagged, Scott Brinker, Hala Taha, Tom Fishburne, Kotryna Kurt, and Mark Metry and they commented on the post. I didn't just randomly tag them; I had an existing relationship with them. Each of these people has a huge following and more importantly, followers who are marketers, sellers and startup founders.

1,072 people who have the title Salesperson viewed your video

Founder	660
Marketing Specialist	571
CEO / Executive Director	375

The reason it worked is because marketers and sales pros who look up to these brilliant folks, took our content more seriously because their heroes did.

Why do more and more influencers take our content seriously? Our #coffeeconversations is not at all trying to sell anything to organizations. These are topics directed at marketers and we often discuss problems they face on a daily basis.

More importantly the content is conversational, which means our audience can share their approach as to how they made something work. In other words, there's a place for them to comment and showcase themselves, rather than being treated as leads who are sold to.

The Moral of the Story

Identify five key influencers for every piece of content you post on LinkedIn and find a way to get them to interact with you.

Do not tag and SPAM the life out of these people on a regular basis. If you do so, you'll lose their trust and exposure to their audience. If these influencers are important to you, earning and retaining their trust should be even more important.

"Identify five key influencers for every piece of content you post on LinkedIn and find a way to get them to interact with you." #TheGrowthHackingBook #GrowthHackingMovement #GrowthHackingDay

While this information will help you, here's a couple of points to remember:

Engage with every comment you receive, within a certain time frame. Every time there's a comment, your post becomes visible to the connections of the one who commented. Respond to them but comment on only a few posts at a time so that you can reply to other posts when the engagement starts to dip. This will keep your post on top at all times.

Tag relevant people when you respond. Tag people who are relevant to your content while responding to those who commented on your post, but only when you think the tagged person would add value to the conversation. Otherwise, it becomes a spammy act.

Don't Stick to Only One Type of Content

You've probably heard from peers in the marketing community that native videos really work on LinkedIn. This is so *NOT TRUE*.

There was a time when the LinkedIn algorithm promoted native videos but not anymore. Again, personal experiments show that the more you stick to content in a single format, your visibility comes down.

My Second Content Experiment

After initially discovering that videos were working for me, I only created video content. The first few video posts were getting an average of 4,000+ views by my target audience, but two weeks later it spiraled down.

Then I posted this:

Again, the engagement and the number of views went up. I tried posting more text-only content and again, the engagement started to decline. Finally, after a few more rounds of experimentation, I realized that the more varied forms of content I posted, the more visibility and engagement posts earned.

What I Learned:

Text-only content does well when longer. In terms of videos, the visibility and engagement increases when they are shorter.

Your 1st Degree Contacts Matter

I don't believe that you should connect only the people you know on LinkedIn. LinkedIn is a place to network with peers in the industry. With that being said, be selective when accepting connection requests.

This has a direct impact on how your LinkedIn profile is perceived. The more credible people in your first-degree connections are, the easier it becomes to establish your credibility. This works on the psychology that you are the average of the type of people you hang out with. In other words, your network is your net worth.

LinkedIn makes it easier for you to evaluate your connections. LinkedIn Sales Navigator gives you an SSI score (Social Selling Index score), which works more like your financial credit score. The higher the SSI score of an individual the higher their credibility.

Here's What a Typical SSI Score Looks Like

The SSI score is based on a professional individual brand. It takes a look at how social a brand is, their engagement on LinkedIn and so on. To improve your credibility, it makes sense to connect with people having an SSI score of 54 and above. Think of this like a movie, which has an IMDB score of more than six.

Also self-evaluation of your SSI score will tell you exactly where you need to improve to increase your impact on LinkedIn.

The above SSI image tells you that there's room for improvement in the following areas:

Engagement: Engaging with content posted by others, sharing valuable content, etc.

Finding the Right People: Making more targeted connections.

Brand Establishment: Opportunity to make your profile more relevant and meaningful to your target audience and more.

Hacks are Temporary, Commitment is Permanent

Every time there's a hack found, it comes with an expiration date. Social platforms keep changing their algorithms. We're in the times of AI where you can expect the algorithms of social platforms to change and be tweaked every hour. Don't just commit to the tactics, commit to the principles of hacking your way to creating an impactful presence.

My guiding principle is, "make a difference in the lives of the people you want to impact in a positive way". LinkedIn may throw a wrench into the hacks once in a while but it will never damage your plan if you have a clear goal.

Circumstances may slow things down occasionally, but there's no stopping.

AUTHOR BIOGRAPHY

Yaagneshwaran Ganesh, often referred to as Yaag, is among the top 100 Global Martech Influencers, is a TEDx Speaker, a member of the Forbes Council and the author of five books. He's a speaker across business forums such as CII Young Indians, Chamber of Commerce Netherlands, Kerala Startup Mission (Initiative by the Government of Kerala), and academic institutions such as IIT's, Saxion University of Applied Sciences and more.

He's an active member of the startup ecosystem and is part of the Google for Entrepreneurs initiative "Startup Weekend", and a sounding board for startups in APAC and Europe.

Yaag, also writes columns for HuffingtonPost, Forbes, Martech Series, Martech Advisor, dtNEXT, Techstory, ManagementNext and more.

Where to Find Yaagneshwaran
www.linkedin.com/in/yaagneshwarang

"Crack the content consumption game on LinkedIn."

Influencer Marketing: Getting Results Via A Data Driven Process

By Ishaan Shakunt

What Is It?

If social media marketing, affiliate marketing and paid display ads had a baby, it would be influencer marketing. It has a lot of the positives and negatives of the three combined.

This channel especially is amazing because it is so diverse and is giving opportunities to so many emerging young entrepreneurs. If done right, this can give you much better ROI than other marketing channels; if not done right, it can be a huge waste of your time and money.

Influencers are people who have already built communities or following in a particular niche. You collaborate with them to share your message with their audience.

Why Does It Work?

To build their communities and following they need to consistently post good content in a particular niche. Their audience is interested in the niche and chose to follow them because of this content.

- **Trust:** Associating with great influencers makes their audience trust and like your brand since they trust and like the influencer.

- **Targeting:** You can actually target your customers based on the type of influencers, primarily based on their niche and location.

- **Trend:** Since multiple well-followed people post about your message and may even nudge other people to do so, it becomes a trend, which often leads to virality.

- **Timeless:** All the posts from your campaign stay in the influencers' profiles and people often check out the influencers' old posts.

Even though influencer marketing is growing extremely fast, I still believe it is uncluttered and less competitive than most other marketing channels out there.

It is so effective that Instagram itself has considered adding features, which will take influencer marketing one step further, on its platform.

Who Is It For?

Influencer marketing works best for industries like food, fashion, fitness and consumer packaged goods (CPG), etc.

This is because it is easier to get creative influencer marketing ideas for the products and services, which can be shown visually in a post.

Due to the type of influencers on Instagram, it is easier to target the potential buyers of these products.

There are numerous case studies where it has worked wonders for other brands as well. It is arguably one of the most creative marketing channels out there. You just need to understand it, get creative with it and test it out.

Just think about it. If Instagram ads can work extremely well for software companies, why not for influencer marketing? It's on the same platform and has less competition.

Process - How To Do It Effectively

Here are some things I want to talk about:

1. Setting KPIs
2. Campaign Design
   a. Content
   b. Influencers
   c. Pricing
3. Tracking
4. Analyzing
5. Bonus: Taking it forward

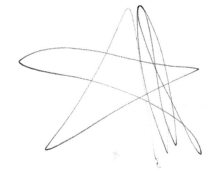

So let's get straight into it.

KPIs: How to Measure Your Marketing Success

What should be your marketing goals for Influencer Marketing: Likes, Positive Comments, Reach?

That was a trick question. Your marketing goal doesn't change with a channel. It remains the same. Broadly it can be one of two goals:

1. Awareness
2. Leads

The right key performance indicators (KPIs) help you understand whether your marketing efforts are actually mapping to your goal or not. What are the right KPIs for you then?

For influencer marketing, your primary KPI should almost always be **engagement**.

1. If your Marketing goal is brand awareness, your KPIs can be reach, engagements, number of posts, etc. If someone looks

at the posts that are a part of your marketing campaign and connects with them, that person is very likely to engage with the post. If your posts have a high reach and low engagement that may mean that something went wrong; maybe the posts didn't click with your customers or you didn't select the influencers with the right audience.

2. If your marketing goal is getting leads, your KPIs can be engagement, clicks, website visits, purchases, etc. People who engage with your content have already shown some amount of intent that they like your product. Measuring engagement or clicks both work well in this case. Other metrics like website visits and purchases may vary a lot due to other factors like your site speed, your website's conversion rate, etc.

"Your marketing goal doesn't change with a channel. It remains the same. Broadly it can be one of two goals: 1. Awareness and 2. Leads." #TheGrowthHackingBook #GrowthHackingMovement #GrowthHackingDay

IMPORTANT - How do you get higher engagement?

The engagement you get from a campaign will depend on the following things:

- Number of influencers
- Number of followers they have
- Their engagement rate
- How engaging your content is
- How many people (apart from your influencers) take part in the

campaign and post organically

- The engagement these organic posts get

I'll cover each of these points in the upcoming sections, so keep rea
(Bossy much?)

Creatives: What Should You Promote?

Keep your marketing objectives in mind. What do you want to communicate to your audience and what action do you want them to take?

Here is a list of things to focus on:

1) Message

Have you ever seen an ad that was amazing and memorable but you just don't remember the brand and what they were trying to promote? Influencer Marketing is highly susceptible to this, being such a creative channel.

Make sure what you want to communicate is not lost in your creative genius.

2) Inclusion

Inclusion basically means trying to get potential customers to take some action so that they are a part of the campaign.

Most of the posts that have high engagement or even go viral are posts that have something in them that pushes people to either tag their friends or share it with someone.

The content may be enlightening, relatable, interesting or amusing.

Don't forget to ask people to take action. One way you can do this effectively is by running a competition.

Taking action (like taking part in a competition by sharing a post for you) has lesser friction than buying your product. If you can convince

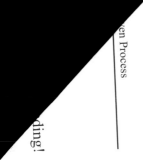

you, they are more likely to convert and your
ople.

t metric that has a massive affect on the
d is one of the things that can lead to virality.
inclusion.

When you pay an influencer to post for you, you are paying for the engagement and the business you will get because of that influencer. If your campaign has a competition which people can take part in, you will get additional engagements and benefits from these organic posts.

To illustrate the power of repostability, I created the chart below.

% of paid engagement: What percentage is the organic engagement in comparison with paid engagement?

Eg: 10 paid and 5 organic will be 50%. 10 paid and 20 organic will be 200%.

Repostability: What % of people, who engage with your posts, also take part in your competition.

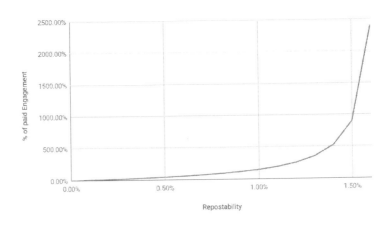

Try to get as many people as possible to take part in your campaign organically. The values in this graph may vary if we change different factors (like budget, industry, demographics, etc.) but this can give you a really good idea of the impact of this metric.

4) CTA

Tell people viewing your posts exactly what action you want them to take. This is essential for all marketing activities as this reduces the mental effort required for them to take action.

5) Brand Image

Make sure that the post is in line with your brand image. Colors, graphics, themes, messaging, everything.

6) Trackability

You will have to track the performance of your posts. (More in section below)

To track your campaign's posts, add a hashtag that's unique to your campaign.

So, who makes the creatives?

a) **You create a picture and share it with the influencers.**

   i) This is actually the easier option to implement. On the other hand, it is very difficult to create something that every influencer's audience will enjoy and relate to.

b) **They create a picture/video based on how you instruct them and incorporate their own creativity and style into it.**

   i) Try including as many things as you can to make sure you are communicating your instructions properly. You can add the following to your documentation:

   (1) Instructions

   (2) What is not acceptable

(3) Moodboard and Examples

(4) Hashtags

(5) Product placement Instructions

(6) Approval

Influencers: Finding the Right Influencers For You

Influencers are the core of any Influencer marketing campaign! So much so that they're even in the name "Influencer Marketing" *(Bad joke?)*

Macro and Micro Influencers

I want to start with this because they are extremely different from each other and businesses would want to use either of them.

	Micro Influencers	Macro Influencers
Followers	Lesser (<25,000)	More (>25,000)
Negotiation	Lesser	More
# Influencers/ Campaign	More	Less
Cost / Influencer	Lesser	More
Targeting	Better	Wider
Their image with followers	Trust their opinion on things in their niche	Look up to what they do in their niche
Effect on brand image	Personal Level	Grand Level
Availability	A lot of them	Much lesser
Engagement Rate	Higher	Lower

Niche

A niche is what they post about. What would their followers expect them to be an expert in? Here are some examples of niches: Food, Fashion, Technology, etc.

Select the influencers whose content, you think the people who are interested in your brand might follow, i.e. whose followers are mostly your brand's target audience.

It's usually a bad idea to go after influencers who try to be in more than 2 niches since their image isn't very clear in the minds of their followers.

Engagement rate

We've already established that engagement is a really important metric and probably will be one of the primary KPIs for your influencer marketing campaigns.

The average engagement rate of an influencer tells you out of the followers that he or she has, what percentage do usually engage with their posts.

How do you know what a good engagement rate is? Well, this depends primarily on three things:

1. The Region
2. The Number of Followers
3. The Niche

For your reference, here is a Followers vs Engagement Rate graph that I created by analyzing over 1000 Indian Instagram influencer profiles.

Shoutout to my friends at InfluenceMonk, Influencer Marketing Agency, for providing me with the data.

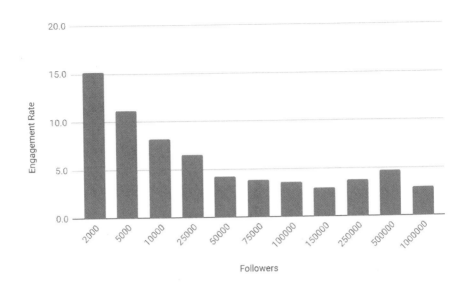

Check for inappropriate content

A lot of pages on Instagram have gained popularity by featuring very racy or inappropriate pictures, which don't align with most brand images. There might be other inappropriately innovative things people do on Instagram to gain followers. Do look at the influencers' posts to see whether or not they are a correct fit for your brand.

Fake influencers

Around 35% of all influencer profiles that we analyzed were fake. *Read that again.*

This is huge! This means that having fake influencers isn't something you can just ignore anymore.

People can buy followers and engagement illegally on Instagram for low costs.

These services have created a lot of fake accounts, which are run by bots. Whenever someone buys followers, these bots just go ahead and follow that account.

How does this impact your marketing campaign?

If you pay someone who just buys followers, their engagement rates will be almost nothing.

But, if you pay someone who has bought followers and then also engagement, you will get high engagement from that influencer but this engagement won't contribute to your marketing goals.

How to check whether an influencer is buying followers?

You can use a free tool like app.influencemonk.com to check the number of followers any influencer has had at different intervals of time. If you see any spikes followed by a fall in the number of followers, you can assume that the influencer is fake or at least suspicious and try to avoid him or her, or dig into it further.

If all the comments on an influencer's posts seem too generic and maybe a lot of them are also out of context, then you can assume that they are buying engagement.

Influencer's connection with followers

Especially when you are working with macro influencers, you should check how well the influencer is connecting with their followers by replying to comments on posts, videos and stories of their lives.

There have been multiple cases where people partnered with a macro influencer but haven't seen any significant successes just because the followers of that influencer didn't really connect with him or her.

This is a much smaller issue when you are working with micro influencers since they have a small following making it easier to relate to and trust them.

Influencer's brand

Again, especially when working with macro influencers, you can check whether or not the influencer's brand resonates with your brand image.

Example: If you are a company that focuses on creating eco-friendly products then you can try looking for influencers who have posted about environmental issues before.

If your brand has a masculine image, you can try looking for influencers who also have portrayed a masculine image of themselves.

Pricing: How Much Should You Pay the Influencers?

Look at your business goals and determine the right KPIs. Estimate how you can pay for those KPIs to get profitable results then try achieving them for a much lower price.

Example

Business goal: Store walk-ins

KPI: Engagement

Assumption: If I get 100 engagements on my posts, 1 person will visit my store.

Average order amount from my store is 200$.

Based on my profit margins and business requirements, I can pay 50$ per store walk in.

So I can pay 50$ for 100 engagements, i.e. 0.5$ per engagement.

Now look at the influencers you were looking to work with and try and predict how much of your KPI you can generate working with them. Try and negotiate with them, if they can't agree to work at your acceptable price or lower, they might just not be a good fit for you.

If you're taking advantage of repostability *(which you should)*, you will also have to account for how much organic engagement you may get. This calculation can get a little complicated, you can consider taking consultation from an influencer marketing agency.

Tracking: What should You Monitor Once the Campaign is Live and How?

1. Tracking metrics on an influencer level is very important. You can use various techniques like giving different links to different influencers, giving different promo codes or using UTM parameters:

    a. Try tracking the following Influencer Side:

        i. Did they post it at the correct time?

        ii. Is the post graphic/video is in sync with your guidelines?

        iii. Did they take it down before the campaign ended?

        iv. Did they post something right after posting your post?

        v. Did they use the right CTA and hashtag?

    b. Performance Side:

        i. Track all the KPIs that you had chosen at the start of the campaign as frequently as you can.

2. Comments:

    a. See what people are commenting. Take insights and respond to them as soon as possible.

    b. If your message got taken in a wrong way decide whether or not you should immediately stop the campaign.

Analyzing: How to Read and Understand the Results?

1. Your funnel: See where most people dropped off from your marketing funnel.

2. Did you get great engagement but extremely few people

visited your website? Try including a better CTA next time or providing a better incentive for people.

    a. Did you get a lot of traffic to your website but people didn't convert as well? Do some conversion rate optimization on your website. Try seeing which type of influencers gave better results and use more of those influencers.

3. Best Influencers: See which influencers performed better.

    a. Maybe some influencers got you a great amount of engagement but the traffic coming from them isn't enough.

4. Understand your audience better: See where most of your results are coming from.

    a. Which influencer gives the most engagements, who gives the most clicks, whose followers are converting better on your website, etc.

5. Gather real feedback: People are extremely comfortable with expressing their thoughts in the comments. You can use this as real feedback for your marketing campaign and your company.

Bonus: Taking it Forward

1. Now that the campaign is over and you have analyzed the results, you can use this data to run much better campaigns the next time and onwards.

2. You can boost influencers' posts if you think the content is good and gave good results. Since it will help them gain visibility as well, most influencers will agree to this.

3. You can also try and buy the rights to the post content to use as marketing collateral for your other campaigns.

AUTHOR'S BIOGRAPHY

Ishaan Shakunt is a Growth Marketing Specialist. He primarily handles SEO and CRO and contributes to other marketing channels at HighRadius Corporation. He is a Research Partner at InfluenceMonk.

Ishaan started his marketing career by convincing restaurants and coaching institutes around his college to hire him. He consulted various startups to help create the right marketing plan for a smooth launch and lasting success. He has worked with multiple startups as a freelancer, member and intern.

Ishaan created and tested multiple concepts primarily around marketing. He took multiple training sessions on personality development, digital marketing and personal branding for over 1500 people.

Where to Find Ishaan
www.linkedin.com/in/ishaan-shakunt

"Around 35% of all influencer profiles that we analyzed were fake. This means that having fake influencers isn't something you can just ignore anymore."

Instagram Growth: 0 To 10K Followers In 3 Months

By Vivek Agrawal

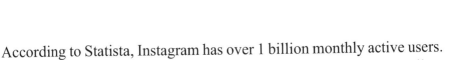

According to Statista, Instagram has over 1 billion monthly active users. This number is growing at a steady pace, which makes it an excellent platform for marketers. Instagram's Ad Revenue is expected to reach over $10 billion in 2019.

Instagram is famous among the younger generation, and hence, Instagram enjoys the highest rate of engagement among other social media platforms. On Instagram, engagement with brands is 10X higher than Facebook and over 80x higher than Twitter.

The top 3 countries in terms of Instagram users are the United States, Brazil, and India. Hence, Instagram marketing has great potential for business. Here is the step-by-step method that has helped me grow my client's accounts organically on Instagram, and how you can do it too!

Step 1: Market Research

One of the critical factors that determine the failure/success of a business is either its coherence or its uniqueness in the market. If you try to sell something that isn't in demand by the local audience, you are potentially wasting a lot of time, effort, and money. However, you are likely to see positive results if you are catering to the needs of your target audience.

Hence, to become successful in your work, you first need to find the right platform, right audience, proper choice of words, correct packaging of the product, and so on.

The first step to growing your Instagram followers is market research. Here are the things that you should research during this phase.

- Competitors' Accounts
- Local Instagram Accounts
- Hashtags to be used
- Type of Graphic/Video to create
- Current trends in the target area
- Keywords that influence user behavior
- Target Audience Demographics

Accumulate the following metrics in a spreadsheet to form a plan to execute:

- Total posts
- No. of Followers
- Total Following
- Instagram Bio
- Website Links

All of these statistics can then be interpolated with data collected on each day to make it into useful information. This interpolation allows you to get a snapshot of the activities that were done on those accounts.

A simple subtraction of the numbers gives you an idea of the growth rate in terms of Posts, Followers, and Following of these influential accounts in your niche.

This data can be used to understand trends in a particular industry.

Step 2: Create a Monthly Calendar

Based on the data collected for a week from the previous step, you can plan a posting schedule. Here is the information you require:

- Frequency of Posting - No. of posts per day & week
- Four sets of Hashtags created to maximize reach & impressions
- Type of Content that the Target Audience likes
- Caption ideas
- Keywords for Alt Text

Create at least five buffer posts. It is essential on Instagram to post almost daily. Instagram gives importance to content creators and businesses who are active on their platform. Hence, the buffer posts can be used in cases when it is not possible to generate new content.

Your competitor is posting daily and is showing up on your audience's feed. If you skip a day, or a few days, your audience sees more of your competitor and less of yours. The downside is that your audience is more likely to engage with your competitor. This will also give Instagram the signal that your audience wants to see more of your competitor than you, so your content is more likely to get bumped down in the future.

You can either upload your posts manually on specific times or use post scheduling service providers such as Later, Hootsuite, Buffer, PostCron. Automated posting has the advantage of scheduling once and forgetting about posting. The downside is that once scheduled; you are less likely to make any changes or make use of the current market trends. So, be wise and make a rational decision about posting.

Step 3: Optimize the Current Profile

The reason for marketing on Instagram is that people come to visit your profile and enjoy seeing it. Since Instagram is a visual medium, it would make the most sense if what someone sees is pleasing to the eyes.

Whatever steps one takes (Except Ads & Stories) to grow an account on Instagram, is to direct the traffic to their Instagram profile. Hence, all your growth efforts will go to waste if you do not have a great face to put on when someone visits your profile. Once the user is on your profile, they have a few actions they can take:

- Open your website
- Call you
- Email You
- Find Directions to you
- Interact with your Posts/Stories/Highlights

As they say, the first impression is the last impression, and it is valid for Instagram marketing too. When someone opens your profile, you have about 3 seconds to catch their attention. Making sure that every element is optimized to grab your audience's eyeballs is very crucial. Using online tools such as LingoJam, one can create stylish looking fonts for Instagram Bio to grasp the user's attention.

As soon as someone opens your Instagram profile, they see the following:

- Your profile name
- Your profile image
- No. of posts
- No. of followers
- No. of following
- Bio (Optional)
- The website link (Optional)
- Call to actions such as Email/Call/Directions (Optional)

Make sure to create a likable profile that gives off significant social signals. If you do not have a business account, convert your profile into a business account.

Maintain healthy followers/following ratio.

Your Instagram profile is like a landing page and so design your landing page to get the maximum viewers to like and engage with the profile and possibly send a DM or navigate to your website.

Changes must on the background and not just the foreground. Change the "Alt Text" of your posts to make them more friendly to differently-abled people as well as to the search engines.

Adding a little bit of metadata allows our profiles to be more easily searchable by Instagram.

"You do not have to be perfect to be the best, you just have to be one step ahead of the rest." TheGrowthHackingBook #GrowthHackingMovement #GrowthHackingDay"

Step 4: Engage with the ideal audience

Next step is, engaging with the ideal audience.

Here are a few ways to be seen by your target audience on Instagram:

- Hitting the Explore Page
- Getting noticed on Suggestions
- Finding on Search/Hashtags
- Ads
- Tagging
- Follow/Like/Comment
- Shout-outs
- Location Tagging

and so on.

Explore page is influenced by Instagram algorithm; you have less control over its results. The same applies to Suggestions. The amount of traffic/attention you can get by Hashtags depends on the time you post, as well as the competition for that particular hashtag.

The thing that you can control is tagging and engagement. You have full control over who you tag in your posts, who you follow, and whose posts you like/comment.

When you run Ads, you trust Instagram to show your content to the most relevant audience. If however, you have a list of accounts that you think are your target audience, you can engage with them.

Start engaging with your target audience via likes, comments, follow, etc. along with getting shoutouts, and engagement exchange. This allows you to increase your reach, and be seen by more people. Instead of using generic comments, post comments that are relevant to the post.

Once you start engaging with the target audience, the audience begins engaging back since you have found them based on their preferences. This way, not only you start growing your followers, but also start getting more likes, comments, shoutouts, and so on.

Step 5: Analytics

Instagram comes with a bunch of options for you to know about your account as well as get feedback about your marketing efforts. When it comes to improving on Instagram, Instagram Analytics is your best friend! This is a side of Instagram that needs to be opened daily to know about the growth.

On the Activity tab, you can have a look at all the information about Interactions taken on your account, as well as the Discovery of your account.

On the Content tab, you can see specific information about each post and story. You can see metrics such as Calls, Comments, Emails, Engagement, Follows, Get Directions, Impressions, Likes, Profile Visits, Reach, Saved, Shares, Texts, and Website clicks. This data is highly crucial to understand how your content is performing.

On the Audience tab, you see the demographics of your audience to know the health of our audience and if you are attracting the right kind of audience to your page. You can see the Location, Age range, Gender, and active timings of our followers. This allows us to make changes to our marketing campaign and optimize our posting time, area, and so on.

Also, track the performance of individual posts. The "View Insights" button comes below every post of an account. There, you can see the no. of Impressions that a post gets and what are the sources of that impression. Your target should be to get most of your views from Home because if someone sees your post on their home, it means they are your loyal followers.

Create content that is share-worthy and engaging to your target followers. It is easy to get fake likes, however, is tough to get real engagement from real people who enjoy seeing the content that you share. This is the reason that the one metric that you should try to increase always is the no. of shares and saves. The higher number of shares sends a positive signal to Instagram because if someone is sharing your content, it means it has some value.

You can start implementing NOW!

Irrespective of your niche, you can use this 5-step method to grow your Instagram account from 0 to 10K in 3 months.

Instead of relying on other service providers to automate your tasks, you can take charge and do it all yourself. You can automate all repetitive actions using free tools at www.agrawalvivek.com and grow organically on Instagram!

AUTHOR BIOGRAPHY:

Vivek Agrawal is a graduate from Manipal University and has a strong background in IT. Due to his expertise in coding, he has been very productive in creating automation tools for Instagram, YouTube, Facebook, Google Drive, etc.

During his first job at EduPristine, he was responsible for managing PPC Ads for the company. While working, he noticed his colleagues copying and pasting the same message over and over again to different people. He was taken aback for a while and thought that it is a computer's task to do automated tasks, not a human's. So, he took 3 days and created a tool using iMacros (a browser automation extension) to automate the entire lead generation process. The lead generation team now had to just input the message to send and the tool would do the rest of their work!

This automation using freely available extension inspired him to create even better tools for Social Media automation. This urge to automate on social media led him to start his own venture - AV Tech global - a digital marketing venture. He now works as a Social Media Growth Strategist for Makeup and Fashion artists to grow them on organically Instagram. Since Vivek believes that computers are designed to do automated work and humans should spend time doing creative work, he provides most of his tools for free on his website.

In his spare time, Vivek loves to play Music and help people with mental disorders such as Anxiety, Depression, Mania, etc. He has successfully counseled people out of 3+ years of Depression in less than 4 weeks without any medication. He writes about mental health, Meditation,

Music, and his other hobbies on Quora.

Where to Find Vivek
www.agrawalvivek.com
facebook.com/access2vivek
www.quora.com/profile/Vivek-Agrawal-98

"If you have to repeat the same task multiple times - Optimize it OR automate it. If not, you are just wasting your time."

TACTICAL SKILLS

"Customers don't expect you to be perfect. They do expect you to fix things when they go wrong."

DONALD PORTER

THE SCIENCE OF WRITING A BESTSELLING BOOK

By Parul Agrawal

At some point in their life, 85% of people want to write a book and only 1% of them end up publishing one. Among this 1%, only a small percentage of Authors are able to create the right impact and strike a chord with their readers. So what puts some Authors ahead in the game compared to others?

After helping over 150 writers write, publish, launch and market their books I have come to the consensus that along with a great message, authors need to have a solid platform and work on their branding. In this chapter, I will cover the Why and How of building an author platform to grow your business, sell more books and create an impact with your message.

The Why?

Branding is about having a consistent message, delivering it clearly, connecting with the audience emotionally and then motivating them to buy our products and services.

Think for a moment – would you buy a product that has not been consistently marketed to you?

Most likely not!

The same principle applies to Authors. You have written a great book, there's no doubt about it. But why will anyone apart from your friends and family buy it? Do they know you? Do they trust you? Why should they care?

Trust

Writing a good book is one part of the puzzle and sometimes the easiest piece. If you have a good product, people will be curious to investigate it, but reaching out to the right audience and having them click on the buy button needs some extra work.

That's where Author branding comes into the picture. It's creating an image, a consistent identity so your readers start recognizing you. We all know Stephen King is a suspense author and J.F. Penn writes thrillers.

Working on your online and offline presence, showing your authentic self to readers, sharing regularly about your book progress – the highs and lows, all help with building trust among your fans.

Standing Out From the Crowd

The number of books being published in the U.S. and the World has exploded. Bowker reports: over one million books were self-published in 2017. Since 2012, the number of ISBNs assigned to self-published titles has grown by 156 percent.

With so much noise, how can authors position themselves and distinguish their work from others in their genre?

Today, using the power of social media, Authors can tap into the emotions of readers and provide them with an overall experience that their competition is missing. Sharing articles, whether on your personal blog or outside publications, being interviewed on various podcasts, collaborating with other authors from the same or different genres, and being a cheerleader during their book launch will put you in front of new readers who will eventually become your dedicated fan base.

Changing Publishing Landscape

Marketing themselves is of utmost importance for self-published authors to sell their books; but, with a changing publishing scenario, it's becoming important for authors trying to pitch their book for traditional publishing. Traditional publishers will pay more attention to you if you have a following, a community that loves your work. Such a following comes with strong branding: your book genres, your book covers, your social media presence, your website, your logo, your headshot – everything should consistently remind your readers about you, even in their sleep. As Jeff Bezos says, "A brand is what other people say about you when you're not in the room." Now, that is some branding!

Branding Helps You Sell

If you are serious about building a career as an Author, then you need to focus on branding yourself. Effective branding serves as the foundation that attracts the right readers and opportunities to you. Building your reputation as an Author can put you on a pedestal as a speaker, coach and an expert in your field/genre, thus bringing you multiple sources of revenue.

As an Author, you want to just write, but if you want to create an impact with your books and share your message with a wider audience, then you must focus on branding.

The root term in the word "Authority" is "AUTHOR"!

"If you want to create an impact with your books and share your message with a wider audience, then you must focus on branding." #TheGrowthHackingBook #GrowthHackingMovement #GrowthHackingDay #GrowthHacking

The How

So now that we know that we need to brand ourselves as Authors, the most important question that comes to mind is how to establish ourselves as an Author.

Gone are the days when Authors had to submit their manuscript to multiple publishers and wait in anticipation for a phone call. Self-publishing has made it a breeze for authors to reach their readers. However, we need to implement some important aspects to make sure our book is well received.

Know Your Why

One client of mine wanted to use her book as a business card and ended up making over six figures by up-selling her program based on the book. Another client wanted to write a book solely to honor her grandfather. She ended up earning the respect and love of her family and community – this was priceless for her. Each Author has different goals with their book. To define the structure of your book and communicate your message at a deeper level, knowing your intention behind writing the book is of vital importance.

Mind Map Your Book

A mind map is a visual representation of ideas and how they all relate to one another. Mind maps are great for brainstorming ideas, keeping organized, and can help you make progress in writing your book. Here's how it works:

- In the center of a paper draw a circle and write your book's central idea.
- Draw another circle on the side of the paper and write the first idea that comes to your mind inside the circle. This is your first sub-topic. Connect both circles.
- Repeat this process for 7-12 subsections while connecting your side circles to the main circle.
- Next, repeat this process for each subtopic and come up with

an additional 5-10 sub-subtopics.

- Convert each subtopic into a chapter heading and each sub subtopics into subheading for your chapters.
- Arrange the subheading as your Table of Contents.

Below is an example of the outline after your mind map:

A. INTRODUCTION

B. CHAPTER 1

B.1 JUICING BASICS

- What is Green Juice
- Why Green Juice

B.2 What are the Benefits of Green Juices

- Fresh juice vs. packaged juice
- Juicing vs. blending

B.3 Why not just eat raw or cooked produce

B.4 How much juice can I drink daily?

C. CHAPTER 2

C.1 WHAT'S IN A JUICE

C.2 Carbohydrate

- Macronutrients
- Micronutrients

C.3 Protein

- Complete Protein

- Incomplete Protein

C.4 Fat

- Saturated Fat
- Unsaturated Fat

C.5 Vitamins

- Fat soluble vitamins
- Water soluble vitamins

Voila! You have just outlined your book, all you need to do is fill in the sections and work on your manuscript.

The Importance of Editing

Finishing your book is a big achievement. Congratulations!

After writing, rewriting and rereading the manuscript multiple times, our brain automatically starts seeing what it expects to see while missing the important details. That is where an editor comes into the picture. A good editor does much more than fix grammar; he or she improves a book's content and structure in a way that preserves the Author's style. Having your book edited from a professional editor (rather than a friend or relative) is worth every penny as your book will be able to stand up to the tough scrutiny from your critics and beloved readers.

Focus on the Presentation

Your book is your window to the world. Before you hit the publish button it is important to make sure that your book is formatted properly and has a beautiful cover. A book cover is the first impression of your book on the reader and one of the most important marketing tools. An unprofessional, homemade-looking cover will not compel the reader to buy the book. Make sure you have a professional designer to help you with your book cover.

Choose your Publishing Platform

The various platforms available to Authors today can be categorized as traditional publishing, hybrid publishing and self-publishing. I love the self-publishing or print-on-demand (POD) platform for its ease of use and transparency when it comes to royalties.

The two most popular platforms for self-publishing are:

Kindle direct publishing (www.kdp.amazon.com):

Kindle direct publishing (or KDP) is a self-service website that allows anyone to publish both ebooks and paperback books for free. With KDP, you get to keep control of your rights and set your own list prices. You can make changes to your book at any time. Compared to other platforms, KDP takes the smallest percentage of your royalties.

IngramSpark (www.ingramspark.com):

Ingram Book Group is the largest distributor and wholesaler of books in the United States. IngramSpark, one of Ingram's most successful divisions, provides print on demand book printing services and an online ebook publishing tool with the world's largest ebook distribution. IngramSpark also offers both hardcover and paperback cover options and hence a preferred choice for many Authors. IngramSpark academy offers various free online courses that Authors publish confidently like a pro with little to no assistance. This platform is always improving and coming out with new ways to help authors, hence it is my personal favorite for publishing books.

Once you know your preferred platform all you need to do is upload your manuscript and cover, then set the right keywords and categories and plan your perfect launch.

Create your Book Launch Strategy

If you Google "book launch" you will come up with thousands of ideas. Knowing where to focus your time and marketing budget is important. There is no right or wrong way when it comes to book promotion but the steps listed below will help you regardless:

- Buy your domain url (example: www.mybook.com). Create a beautiful landing page for your book promotions. Include a book description, cover, author bio, sign up form and a way for readers to contact you on this page.

- Identify and plan what social media channels you want to use to reach your audience. Choose 2-3 channels to get started and share about your book here.

- Blog about your area of expertise and post book excerpts on your personal blog and as a guest blogger on other blogs and publications.

- Show your readers behind the scenes of your book writing/ publishing process and get them involved by asking for their opinion on the book title, cover and other aspects.

- Get interviewed on various podcasts and talk shows to inform readers about your book.

- Reach out to your friends, family members and colleagues and invite them to be a part of your book launch.

- Decide on a launch day and do a massive social media campaign around the launch week.

- Arrange online blog tours and spotlights to gain online visibility for your book.

- Contact local bookstores and libraries to arrange book signings and readings.

Most importantly, don't shy away from promoting your own work. You know you have written a great book and now it's time for you to share your message with the World.

Writing a good book is only one part of the puzzle, marketing it to reach the right audience is a different ballgame. Using the right strategy and focusing on your branding even before you start writing your first word can help you as an Author, to stand out from the crowd and market your book to be a bestseller.

AUTHOR BIOGRAPHY

Parul Agrawal is an Author, Bestseller Launch Expert, Talk Show Host and Forbes Coaches Council Member. She holds two Master degrees in Engineering from Arizona State University (ASU); worked as a Research Scientist at ASU and Engineer for Intel Corporation. In an effort to help others address major medical issues and live more healthily, she pursued holistic studies and acquired her certification as a wellness expert. After launching a successful Wellness Coaching business, Parul delivered the message of health through public speaking in various community centers and corporations.

Parul's life and business changed dramatically after she wrote a book on the benefits of juicing that became an International Bestseller in multiple categories. The book's phenomenal success resulted in her being featured in major publications like the Huffington Post, Thrive Global, Forbes and as a guest on ABC Arizona.

Parul has not only continued her success as an author and businesswoman, but she has paid-it-forward, by helping over 150 writers become bestselling authors, too! She is the CEO and founder of Growth Media AI, an International Publishing and Digital Marketing Platform where she helps thought leaders in the areas of health, wellness and consciousness brand themselves as experts, write their books, achieve bestseller authority status, and land in mainstream media - just like she did! Parul born in India, now lives in Phoenix, United States with her husband and 2 beautiful kids. She also had the honor of being listed as one of the 30 changemakers in India for the year 2018.

Where to Find Parul
www.parulagrawal.com
www.linkedin.com/in/authorparul
www.twitter.com/authorparul

 *"A book cover is the first impression of your book on the reader and one of the most important marketing tools. Make sure you have a professional designer to help you with your book cover."*

A Bird In The Hand: Is Paying Attention Your Greatest Growth Hack?

By Suneet Bhatt

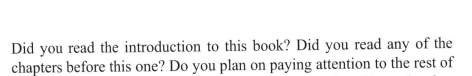

Did you read the introduction to this book? Did you read any of the chapters before this one? Do you plan on paying attention to the rest of this paragraph or are you going to skim directly to a headline,, visual or number below that catches your attention?

We are all time constrained. I am deeply empathetic to people who feel their attention being unabashedly courted and pursued, leaving them with no other option than to skim and accelerate their way through life. It's not like anyone's making it easier for us to focus.

When I worked at Chartbeat, we started using our relationships with media companies to find creative ways to tell stories that capture attention. Our metric, Engaged Time, the time people spent interacting with a piece of content, was directly tied to attention (not to transactional metrics like page views, but on captured, tracked engaged time) and so it made sense. One of my proudest moments running Marketing and Sales was when we collaborated with Farhad Manjoo on this article in *Slate* titled: *How People Read Online: Why you Won't Finish this Article.*

It was amazing that our data was being used to tell a story through a featured columnist in a major publication.

What stuck with me more powerfully was the truth of the article: people weren't paying attention and every day, people were paying less and less attention.

Why Does Attention Matter for Growth?

That was 2013. Now, people have less time, more distractions and as a result, are equipped to pay even less attention.

That's challenging if you're someone in marketing, growth or sales. The funny thing is that for all of our complaints about our customers not paying attention to all the answers and solutions we offer – we're doing them an even greater disservice. We're charged with growing our businesses but we're not spending much time paying attention to our visitors, our readers, and our customers: capturing data, and then testing ideas that would spark that growth.

As individuals charged with growth, we know what we want (marketing ROI, marketing efficiency, competitive advantage), and we also have clarity on what the highest ROI tactic is at our disposal (CRO). Yet what

Neil Patel also learned when he conducted his survey is that only 1.7% of Marketing budgets are allocated to CRO.

We know CRO works.

When Crazy Egg's co-founder, Neil Patel, spoke to 208 companies a short while back (ranging in size from $1mm in Revenue to $291mm in Revenue), they shared unequivocally that the marketing tactic with the highest ROI was CRO.

What Gives?

Much of the tension here can be attributed to what's referred to as "the paradox of happiness." We know what makes us happy long-term (eating well, sleeping well, exercising) and we know them well enough to recite them when queried. When push comes to shove and it's time to act, we'll very often choose the thing that gives us short-term happiness even when we know it's not the right long-term decision.

CRO (Conversion Rate Optimization) is the right long-term decision. CRO is the process by which you monitor, analyze and understand user behavior, then run tests in an effort to optimize user experience toward a goal or an outcome.

"We're charged with growing our businesses but we're not spending much time paying attention to our visitors, our readers and our customers: capturing data, and then testing ideas that would spark that growth." #TheGrowthHackingBook #GrowthHackingMovement #GrowthHackingDay #GrowthHacking

Paying attention is the right long-term decision. It's just not as sexy as a new trend, a new channel or a new buzzword. As a result, it doesn't get celebrated nor does it get prioritized.

We know it's not being prioritized because we surveyed 1350 self-identified Marketing and Growth experts.

When we talk about a bird in the hand (vs. two in the bush), we're referring to the missed opportunities we have right in front of us. A whopping 69% of Marketers are ignoring the bird in the hand: existing visitors, readers, users and customers.

How convinced am I that paying attention is a differentiator? Based on this one single data point, we have proof that if you're paying attention to why people are and aren't hitting their goals, you'll instantly be in the top one third of Marketers. Paying attention is the clearest and easiest way to separate you from two thirds of your competitors. In the context of the MarTech Landscape this means you've just left over 4,000 companies behind, in the dust.

There's nuance to the remaining 69%. Of the remaining 69%, almost half are only doing one thing that qualifies as CRO and 14% are doing absolutely nothing. I'm impressed they took the time to answer honestly. It tells me how strong the competition is for their time and ultimately that's what we heard, people are too busy. A popular answer. In the end, people arrived at the same conclusion in different ways:

Only 42% of Marketers are doing anything, **even just one thing** that would qualify as CRO.

"I am mostly busy throughout the day and do not have time."
"I'd say it's a combination of reasons. One, a lot of the analytics software is costly. Sure some are free or lower cost, but everything adds up. Another is the hassle or being busy with other things on your website."

Superpowers Don't Make a Superhero

Marketers know what to do. But knowing isn't enough. You have to do something with the knowledge you have.

The same thing can be said about paying attention. Paying attention helps you identify what is and isn't working. That knowledge isn't a superpower, that knowledge doesn't make you a superhero unless you apply it and take action against it.

Take the 15 Minute Challenge (aka the Power Quarter Hour)

One common misconception about paying attention: it doesn't actually take a lot of time to be impactful and meaningful. It takes the right timing and it takes the right reinforcement. It's possible.

1) Block 15 minutes on your calendar every week

To start, block aside 15 minutes on your calendar to spend time paying attention to how people are experiencing your website, your application, your products and your brand. Set the meeting as a recurring event at the same time every week.

- Do you want to start your week with inspiration? Reserve time on a Monday morning after you've completed your Monday morning required work (checking email, planning your week, etc.)

- Do you want to reinvigorate yourself mid-week? Reserve time on Wednesday as a way to bridge the start and end of your work week.

- Do you want time to marinate on ideas over the weekend? Close your week with a Friday afternoon block of time. This will give you data to plan in your subconscious over the weekend which you can use to kick off your week when you get in on Monday morning.

2) Spend those 15 minutes paying attention

Pay attention for 15 minutes with the purpose of finding a missed opportunity, an area where people are getting stuck, and with the goal of developing a hypothesis on something to improve. There are thousands of tools out there for you to use to pay attention to how people are experiencing your application. The important thing is that you make the time to pay attention to those experiences. Focus on pages, tools and content that were a meaningful investment of your team's time (new product, primary CTA, payoff feature) and that attract meaningful engagement from your customers (lots of users, viewers, readers). Nailing the right framework and focus upfront ensures you're looking at experiences with volume (traffic, scrolls, clicks) to support, followed by hypotheses to test against.

- Are your primary CTAs aligned to where people are paying attention? One of the biggest and most consistent things we highlight when we consult with a person using Crazy Egg is the power of a Scrollmap (scroll depth) contrasted with a Heatmap (clicks). Put simply, if 100% of people aren't seeing your primary goal for the page (a button, a form fill, a content piece), you haven't designed your page appropriately to align attention to engagement. We see this on everything from landing pages and homepages through to key aspects of a web application or dashboard. At Crazy Egg, we use this to make sure the domain entry CTA on our homepage is aligned with 100% of the people arriving on our homepage.

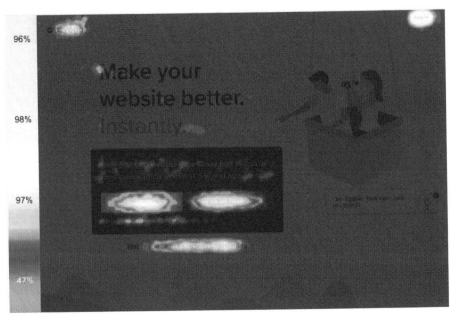

Here you can see that between 97-100% (scrollmap on the left)

of visitors to our homepage are seeing the primary domain entry CTA (primary cluster of clicks on the heatmap).

- Are you watching recordings of people as they make it to and through your most important page? Too often analytics solutions focus on an individual page and don't put that page in the context of an entire website experience. Additionally, while funnel views on their own show averages and high-level flows, there's no substitute for following a user on their actual journey. If you watch Recordings of a user as they work through your site or application to a primary goal page, you'll quickly see where users are getting stuck and what's getting in the way. At Crazy Egg, we used Recordings to completely redesign our JS Installation experience; specifically how we let users check and verify if their JS has been installed correctly (if at all). It's worth noting that we have an exceptionally high JS installation rate; but when we watched the experience, we realized we were confusing customers and burning goodwill for those who managed to succeed despite our design.

- Are you segmenting people based on how they arrive to your site or app? It's incredible what the power of simple filters can do to help you transform your experience. Are people interacting, clicking, or scrolling differently on mobile vs desktop devices? How about new people arriving on your pages for the first time vs those who are returning? Have you segmented clicks and other types of engagement by referrer? I'd assume your paid traffic interacts with your site differently than your organic, which is different again from how someone from a referral partner may interact. At Crazy Egg, we use some 100 segments and filters in the product to quickly see if we can identify different behaviors based on those contexts. We recently spent a lot of time rebuilding our blog and tracking how we refer blog readers to our product by following engagement from different UTM codes.

Each of the above actions (there are others, like polling people on your site and asking them questions) took 15 minutes to analyze and arrive at a hypothesis. We're not looking for hundreds of ideas; instead, this approach is designed to help you find the one, single most impactful thing you can do this week – and then equip you with the data and assets to evangelize that inspiration across your organization.

3) Translate your hypothesis into action

This is the key step: once you harness the inspiration, it's time to take action. There are plenty of tools you can use like the Crazy Egg A/B Testing Tool, to make changes yourself like moving buttons, changing headlines, and repositioning elements on a page without needing a designer or an engineer.

If you do need support to translate your hypothesis onto the page, invite your engineer, designer and other team members to join you on your 15-minute journey each week. Your commitment should be to leave that session with one task to prioritize in the spirit of paying attention to your customers and improving their experience.

Here's the thing: if you embrace Step 2 and focus on the highest investment pages with the highest engagement, you'll undeniably find one clearly inspirational thing you want to test. That's all that matters to put you ahead of the majority of your peers and competition.

As you revisit this cycle each week, your eye for opportunity and your sophistication around what you can execute on will increase as well. You will slowly gain the confidence to identify, extrapolate and test more.

Not because your past tests were all successful, on the contrary; specifically because some weren't and you realized — you still learned something powerful about your audience and their experience that will make you better as a company.

I've run countless failed tests and experiments in my time. I can't think of one that cratered a business. The only ones that had any modest negative effects were the ones I wasn't paying attention to after launch, one's I should have turned off sooner; reminders about the importance of paying attention and that we are always learning.

Do Something

It's too easy to feel informed and smart without doing actual work these days. There's so much content. There are way too many thought leaders (where are all the thought followers?). We've become accustomed to making decisions based on other people's data.

That used to be okay because competition wasn't as fierce. It's not okay today, because now there is too much competition and the people we're trying to serve have higher expectations.

Paying attention to the people who are using your tools, products and services is going to make your business better. Based on the data, it's actually going to put you in a position to leave your peers and competitors behind.

> *"A bird in the hand is worth two in the bush. "*
> *- John Ray (1670)*

AUTHOR BIOGRAPHY

Suneet Bhatt has been a leader in Marketing Technology since 1998 and has had the benefit of taking on, turning around and growing companies in a variety of industries and stages. Most recently, his experiences have led him to a role as General Manager at Crazy Egg, the original Conversion Rate Optimization tool used by hundreds of thousands of websites since 2005. He's also the founder of Dream Village, a startup that uses picture books and the web to help kids explore and address important global issues.

Suneet is a firm believer in the power of paying attention, both professionally and personally. Read his article on the Crazy Egg Blog: *It's Time To Start Paying Attention.*

"Block aside 15 minutes on your calendar at the same time every week, to spend time paying attention to how people are experiencing your website, your application, your products and your brand."

THE POWER OF CUSTOMER RETENTION

by Arun Kumar Sharma

———◆———

"Profit in business comes from repeat customers, customers who boast about your product or service bring new customers."
– W. Edward Deming

Turn Your Customer Into Your Advocate

The Problem

Sam is a small business owner who works hard to bring people to his website and convert them into paying clients.

He's spent a lot of time, money and effort to understand and master the complex procedures related to email, SEO, website design and development, sales funnels, ecommerce, branding, social media, video production and everything else required to attract and convert customers.

He paid large sums of money to trainers, consultants and coaches to learn about acquiring more customers and selling more products.

Sam has experienced much pain from: the breakup of his partnership, having zero social life, missing important family events and twice having absolutely no money in his back account.

After five years of grinding in his business he finally cracked the code to success.

Yes, now people look up to him as a true marketer and entrepreneur who has learned the art of customer acquisition and selling products.

Still, he is not happy and content with his progress.

Why?

Like many other businesses that just manage to survive, Sam ignored one important area. He was content to draw a salary from a hundred customers instead of one employer.

Most of the time the reason for this situation is only one thing, which I call: 'The Great Bucket Leakage'.

The Great Bucket Leakage

Say you're filling up a bucket (your business) with water (new customers and money) and there's hole in the bottom. All the water drains out (losing customers and money).

You're always worried about losing water from your bucket, translates to you're always worried about losing customers and money from your business.

I'm calling this 'The Great Bucket' because you've built this business with so much hard work and hustle, and the leakage makes it frustrating. It means you have to constantly look for new customers.

Growth Hacking is NOT just about bringing new customers into your funnel, it's also about retaining current customers, for a longer period of time.

What's the use of gaining new customers when you're losing them before you can recoup your marketing and operation costs?

Don't overlook the potential for doing more business with your present customers, and focus only on the pursuit of new customers.

Don't be like Sam. With due respect for his work, he was too busy running after new customers and he totally ignored the fact that great and profitable businesses are built on customer loyalty and retention, which are established through creating the best experiences for your customers and increasing repeat purchases.

Why Focus on Customer Retention?

The following studies explain how ignoring this important lesson could lead to the death of your business.

Research from Frederick Reichheld of Bain and Company, shows how a 5% increase in customer retention increases profits by 25% to 95%.

A study by Koyne Marketing shows that existing customers are 50% more likely to try new products and they spend 31% more, when compared to new customers.

Source of Studies: www.invespcro.com/blog/customer-acquisition-retention/

Turn Your Existing Customers into Advocates

Have you ever wondered how customer advocacy works for companies like Apple, Starbucks, Amazon, Royal Enfield and Netflix? Customer advocates are critical to long-term growth for these companies.

Three Stages for Customer to Advocate

Stage 1

Customers are impressed with your best quality products and services, over delivery of promised results and dedication to customer service. Customers are getting to know you; they may have questions and are not yet fully committed.

Stage 2

Personalized deals are offered to your customers, great results and case studies are building. You offer rewards and loyalty bonuses along with continuous excellent service. Customers like and believe in you.

Stage 3

Customers are extremely happy with the results you helped them achieve. They advocate for your company through word of mouth and jump in when you need them most, supporting you however they can. They love your company and tell their friends and people they meet all about it.

At SubMastery Edtech, more than 90% of our customers are repeat buyers. They are responsible for our business sustenance and growth.

Maybe your business is in the early stages and you don't have many clients yet. Focus on customer retention, from day one. Whether you have a small or large base of customers, customer retention needs to be a strategic, innovative and ongoing goal for any business.

Some of these strategies are so simple they are often overlooked. The way to get the best out of this chapter is to go through each strategy and all the hacks mentioned. Highlight the ones you think will work best for your customer, and then implement them.

Although these strategies are oriented towards internet-based businesses like e-commerce, digital information products, and coaching and consulting products and services, many of these hacks will work perfectly for non-internet-based businesses as well.

Three Strategies for Customer Retention

1. Onboarding

Think of onboarding as the very first impression the customer has about your product or service.

It's a very important opportunity for you to develop good rapport with your new customer, to help reinforce that their decision to purchase was right, to set their expectations, and to show them the ways to access support at your company.

Next are ways to help the onboarding process:

Reinforce the Customer's Decision to Purchase

When a customer purchases a product, welcome and congratulate them for their decision. Reinforce that they have made the right decision and remind them how using your product will benefit them.

This could be done over email, with a simple thank-you letter or card and the best, is to send a personal welcome message in video. As your customers see a face behind your brand, they will trust you even more. If you are coaching or running an online course, you can do an onboarding call with your customer to further set expectations, timeline and accountability.

With Screencastify, Loom and similar quick recording tools, it's very easy to send a short 30-second personal video message, which will take about the same time as writing and sending an email.

Tell Your Customer Your Company's WHY

If you can connect with your customer on an emotional level, your relationship will go much deeper. Everyone wants a life with meaning and impact, but most don't know how to go about getting that. If your company's product can prove to be a medium for them to do and spread good, they will happily buy from you.

Let your customers know the Why of your company, the reason for your existence and how your contribution in this world will make it a better place. Linking your products and services with an important purpose is a strategy that many companies build successful businesses with.

Your company's purpose could be a cause for which you really care, it could be related to a welfare activity, environmental protection, helping needy people, building schools, providing education, etc.

Customers feel immense pride to learn they are associated with a company, which has a deep purpose, one who thinks beyond money.

Alpro, a food-based company headquartered in Belgium, heavily promotes a vegan, plant-based diet in an effort to save our planet.

International apparel company TOMS, has run a brilliant 'One for One' initiative for a long time. With every product purchased, TOMS donates one pair of shoes or an equivalent contribution to a cause helping a person in need. Source: www.toms.com/one-for-one-en

Accessibility, Support and Response Time

You should be accessible in case your customer wants to reach you, and where possible, provide 24/7 customer support through email, chat, ticket system and your website's Contact Us page.

Let people know the days and times you are available and the average customer response time. Maintain a customer response time of less than 24 hours.

Use Help Desk support from companies like Zendesk and Freshdesk, and offer online chat options to customers through chat software by Intercom and Help Scout.

Educate Your Customers with an Academy

If your products are SaaS (Software as a Service) or any type of information product, your customers may need support and assistance.

Your customers can benefit if you build training modules around your products and services.

The HubSpot Academy offers a variety of free courses for their products and services, that are open to all.

www.academy.hubspot.com

2. Individualization

How do you feel when someone remembers and calls you by your name? It feels personal, even if it's a computer and technology; it still helps to create a connection.

Every customer is an individual and wants to feel that your communication to them is personal and that it's not generic.

Personalize your communication in such a way that your customer feels taken care of.

Customer Segmentation

If you know the present status and situation of your customers, you can draft your communication to them accordingly. Get to know your customers by paying attention to their behavior, through segmentation surveys, click data, through the pages they visit and their purchase history.

Tag your customers' interests inside your email service account. Active Campaign is a powerful email service that is worth exploring further.

Segmentation tools include Typeform, SurveyMonkey and SurveySlam.

> *"Serve your customers in a way that generates repeat buying, referrals, recommendations, testimonials and great feedback." #TheGrowthHackingBook #GrowthHackingMovement #GrowthHackingDay*

Address Customers by Their First Name

Customers are human beings with a heart and emotions. Powerful bonding can be established when you address your customers by their first name in emails and messages.

Many marketers use their customers' names in the subject line of their emails to create a personal feel and connect with their customers. They do this by simply adding the code {First Name} to the subject line in the draft email and the email software takes care of adding each person's first name.

Another hack is to treat events and festivals as an opportunity to individualize your content for promotions and to encourage repeat purchases. Below is an example of HDFC Bank promoting their product on Mother's Day.

Fig 1: HDFC Bank promotion for Mother's Day using the customer name.

Individual Progress Status

Your customers' progress in any training courses can be sent to them by email on a weekly, or other basis, to remind them how much they have completed and how much work is still pending.

Tools like Teachable, Thinkific and similar Learning Management Systems (LMS) include the feature, *Individual Progress Status*. Integration through Zapier is another option used to automate the *Individual Progress Status* process.

Search Based Email Triggers

A person's sense of urgency and motivation can be used to help them make a purchase decision with search based email triggers and individualization.

Recently I was looking forward to our family trip to a beautiful location and had not yet finalized the hotel booking. I searched online and the very next day I received an email with a discount code for the location and date I had been searching.

Regarding Your Corbett Hotel Search for 18-May

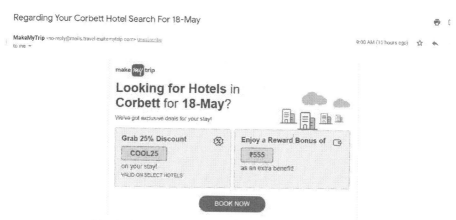

Fig 2: Location based trigger and individualization

Respond to Every Communication

Clients need to feel heard and valued. It's important that you don't miss any genuine doubts and queries from your customers.

If you messed up something, be straightforward and don't write a generic answer. Instead, apologize and make up for your mistake in a way that creates customer satisfaction. Your customers will appreciate this gesture and will see your integrity and will have more confidence in your work.

Customers are using company social media pages to post complaints and questions online and many companies are responding directly to their messages.

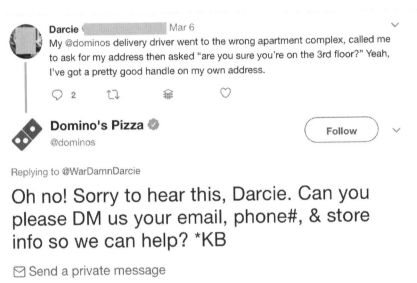

Fig 3: Responding to customer by name in social media.
Source: Domino's Pizza Twitter Stream

According to Dresner Advisory Services' *Business Intelligence Market Study*, it takes 12 positive customer experiences to negate the poor impression left behind from one unresolved or bad experience.

Website and App Language Selection Opportunities

With the help of technology, automatic translation of web pages and apps is possible.

Everybody loves to listen and talk in his or her Mother Tongue. Using vernacular or common styles of languages is becoming popular because they are easier to understand and connect well with customers.

3. Tribe Engagement

Building an engaged tribe around your business has immense benefits for your business success.

When people associate themselves with your brand and feel proud to do so, they become spokespeople and advocates for your company and it's products and services.

Their feedback must be an integral part of your product development process as this can help steer your company in the right direction.

Tribe Engagement Platforms

There are a variety of platforms that can be used to engage your audience, for example Groups on Facebook, Linkedin, Slack and Whatsapp as well as forums.

Control group experience by creating rules of engagement.

In a group setting you can run contests, challenges and activities that keep your followers engaged.

You can also deliver live sessions at regular intervals to help your tribe progress and engage with you, through online tools like GoToMeeting and Zoom.

Social Proof

Social Proof happens when existing customers become aware that your other customers are achieving their desired results, by using your products and services. This enhances their trust of your brand and inspires them to purchase.

Using reviews and testimonials in the beginning of the customer acquisition process helps to create trust and social proof.

It's equally important to keep reminding customers that they can achieve the results they want, just like many others who are achieving their desired results.

Testimonials can be shared through email and social media groups, in advertisements, articles and on websites, on landing pages and in sales funnels.

Membership Benefits

You may introduce membership benefits to your customers. Members feel that they are getting premium benefits by being part of a select group and this helps to increase customer loyalty.

Membership benefits can include discounts and additional benefits. Not everyone will purchase your membership, however frequent users will consider membership if you help them to see its clear benefits.

Alternatively, you can give points with every purchase that can be redeemed for gifts. Many credit card companies do this. E-commerce and travel companies also offer membership benefits.

Fig 4: Travel Portal Make My Trip Membership Benefits

Feedback

Surveys are great for feedback about your products and services.

Make your surveys simple and interesting.

Limit the number of questions you ask as long surveys can be boring and discourage customers from participating.

Ask only one question at a time.

Consider survey tools, Typeform and SurveyMonkey.

Give your customers incentive to complete your survey by sending them free information products and discount coupons. Incentives encourage participation and tell your customers that you appreciate their time and feedback.

Using customer feedback from surveys will give insight on their pain points and will give you the opportunity to create products and services that you are confident your customer wants and needs.

Increase Customer Lifetime Value

Customer Lifetime Value (CLV) is determined by the equation:

Amount of Average Transaction x Annual Purchase Frequency x Expected Years of Relationship = CLV

My marketing friend sold 500 tickets for an event seminar through his Facebook Group. The group had more than 2000 paid members who had purchased his low priced course. Existing customers from the Facebook Group bought 80% of the tickets. This is an example of how the lifetime value of customers can be increased.

Another way to increase CLV is to offer your customers affiliate products like software, courses, coaching and physical products, which can help them get their desired results.

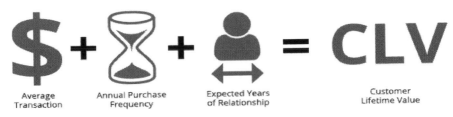

Fig 5: CLV Calculation

Image Source - redrocketvc.blogspot.com/2011/08/lesson-79-determining-customer-lifetime.html

Conclusion

It's critical to retain your customers for the long-term success of your business. Focus on customer retention strategies by including these in your Business Plan.

Treat your customers well. Learn about them with segmentation, wow them with excellent products and services and over-deliver on promised results. Be accessible and answer any doubts and queries quickly. Dedicate the required resources for improving customer ratings and satisfaction. Show your customers that you care for them and are committed to their success. Track their progress, make them a part of your tribe and engage with them at every chance.

Sam Walton's wise words, "There is only one boss. The Customer. And he can fire everybody in the company from the Chairman on down, simply by spending his money somewhere else."

Serve your customers in such a way that generates reciprocity for repeat buying, recommendations and word of mouth publicity. Engage with them, make them feel proud to be a part of your tribe and they'll keep spending money with you.

AUTHOR BIOGRAPHY

Arun Kumar Sharma is the Founder and CEO at education firm, SubMastery Edtech Private Limited. He is a mechanical engineer with 15 years of experience in operations management, business excellence and quality management systems.

Arun has trained more than 15,000 corporate professionals through 700 live trainings. SubMastery has students across the globe, in the niche market for automobile quality professionals.

Arun is author of the activity-based book, *'How to Stay Self-Motivated when Swimming with Sharks'*. His laptop bag always carries one business related book. When at home, he loves spending time with his young daughter who loves to play chess without rules.

Where to Find Arun
www.linkedin.com/in/arunkumarsharma6
www.facebook.com/arunkumarsharma6
www.submastery.com

Know Your Customers

Be accessible, answer questions and address concerns within a quick time frame.

Get to know your tribe better with segmentation and personalized content and communication

Wow them and over-deliver on your promised results to build a engaged tribe around your company

GROWING BUSINESS IN AN UNORTHODOX NICHE

"To be successful, you have to have your heart in your business, and your business in your heart."

THOMAS WATSON, SR., FORMER CEO, IBM

Growth Hack Your Food Business Through Digital Marketing

By Nitish Mathur

———◆———

More than 50% of millennials say that their food and drink purchases are inspired or influenced by the pictures they look at on social media.

With massive digitization happening in our lives, the landscape of food business has been changing tremendously. Now, restaurant, pubs, and food franchises cannot simply rely on the word of mouth to market their restaurants nor are other traditional means like radio or television. Today as a food blogger when I walk into different restaurants, some of them are tapping into digital media and marketing themselves pretty well on social media. But a majority of them are yet to reveal themselves on the social media landscape, and a lot of their presence is quite negligible.

It is a known fact that food business is highly competitive and has a failure rate of more than 50%. If you own a restaurant or a pub, it is extremely important that you level up your marketing efforts and leverage social media and digital marketing to build a strong brand. Being a food blogger I have explored a lot of food outlets across India. I have realized one thing, success in the food business isn't just about serving great food, it is way beyond that.

Here I am listing down nine tips that will help you showcase food lovers what you have got to offer them:

"One of the biggest principles of doing business is adding value to the lives of people. And in the age of social media, you have platforms where you can add value to the lives of people by engaging with them and sharing your kitchen secrets." #TheGrowthHackingBook #GrowthHackingMovement #GrowthHackingDay

1) Get a Website

Your website is your address in the digital space. When you own a website, it opens up a plethora of opportunities and a whole new market of customers. The simple reason being a website makes you discoverable, especially when you publish regular content, do SEO and integrate it with your social media channels. This makes it easy for food lovers to discover you. Yes, putting up a website is a lot of work but believe me when I tell you, nothing comes easy and in the end, it will be all worth it.

2) Leverage Food Bloggers and Influencers

One of the biggest boons of the digital era is you get to connect with people faster. Get connected with local food bloggers and influencers. Invite them to your restaurant, give them discounts on food and in return ask them to share about the great food you serve, to their audience on their social media platforms. That way their audience gets to know you and you get to brand yourself before them.

3) Targeting - Aiming at Decision Makers

Who is the decision maker in the family? The answer to most is — the person who is between 12-25 years old; the children, mostly not married and living with the family.

Many studies were conducted on who the decision makers are, in most of the cases, when it comes to choosing the place to go. One thing, which stood strong, was youths involved in making a plan to go out for a drink or food — crucial and critical.

If the Food and Beverage industry focuses on youth and starts targeting them through social media, this would surely boost business.

4) Sharing Value Via Innovative Ways

One of the biggest principles of doing business is adding value to the lives of people. In the age of social media, you have platforms where you can add value to the lives of people by engaging with them and sharing your kitchen secrets.

With Facebook Live, Dunkin' Donuts got a new opportunity to engage with their biggest social media audience in the most simple and direct ways. Using Facebook live has been such a plus point for Dunkin' Donuts and they now have more followers on Facebook than Twitter and Instagram.

As per TrackMaven, food and beverage industries have the largest audience with the median audience size of 1.8 million.

So, what is the key lesson from this whole Dunkin' Donut leveraging Facebook live episode?

It reveals a bit of you to your customers. Dunkin' Donuts is a global company powered by talented people. Instead of treating their baking process as some kind of secret recipe, they showcased it to their consumers and let them see how their favorite donuts were made.

Marketers can learn a lot from this, you don't always need to give away your secret recipe but your consumers won't mind if you share a few ingredients.

5) Conduct Cool Contests and Giveaways

A lot of holy books say, give a lot to receive more. It holds true when you are building a business. You need to give a lot before you expect something from your customers. Start organizing weekly or monthly contests and giveaways. Start them offline and go live on social media, let your followers see what you are up to and ask participants in the contest to post about the contest. That way you get to reach out to a lot of people building yourself as a brand in the process.

6) Go Completely Social

In the age of foodporn, if you are ignoring the power of social media, you are making a big mistake. People are getting foodgasms seeing mouth-watering pictures of delicacies all over Instagram and Facebook. Brands are sharing their best offers on food and food bloggers are all over, sharing their experiences online. If you want to build yourself as a brand, you need to be a part of this ecosystem. Click the best photos of the best of your food and drinks, then upload them on Instagram and Facebook. Put in 10 to 15 stories each day from your kitchen, serving food, a picture of a happy customer, or whatever about you that is authentic, genuine and a bit flawed. Do the same on Facebook and craft yourself as a social media brand.

That way you will attract food bloggers, influencers and millennials and they won't mind paying a few extra bucks if they loved the content on your account.

7) Get Yourself Listed on Food Apps

Food apps like Zomato and Swiggy have enormously increased the revenue of food outlets as customers can now order their favorite dishes at the press of a button. I personally have seen a lot of food outlets functioning in a small space and making profits selling food via these food apps. If you wish to stay in the food business game, register your restaurant with these food apps. That way you won't lose potential customers who just wish to have some tasty food in the comfort of their home.

8) Tap into Micro Influencers With Social Paying

Word of mouth holds tremendous power even today. A lot of people try out a restaurant at the suggestion of a friend or after seeing a post on social media. I recently went to Cafe Tonino located at Connaught place in Delhi because a friend of mine told me they serve great pizza and their ambiance is wonderful. I featured them in my Instagram story geotagging them and they, in turn, reposted it. So, they got exposure as a restaurant and I got exposure as a food blogger.

When I say social paying, I am proposing a system wherein you allow people with a considerable following, a discount on posting your delicacy on their social media platform or else you can run a contest wherein you will keep track of everyone who posted about you on their social media channel. Maybe after a week or a month, you choose three lucky customers and offer them a free meal.

This idea itself can catapult you as a brand if done properly.

9) Manage Your Online Reputation

Building a brand is easy, maintaining it is the tough part. Nothing can destroy your credibility in food business like a bad review. Would you as a user eat at a restaurant with two-star poor food quality and dead insect reviews? No! Right. You need to make sure that your online reputation always stays intact, otherwise it is just a matter of time before one bad review and it is game over for you.

I am not saying you can completely prevent bad reviews but you can definitely make sure to respond to customer queries and reviews both positive and negative, in a timely and dignified manner. The customer wants to be heard, lend them your ears and respond in a way that portrays you in a positive light. This is what is called online management reputation.

The Final Note

Be genuine and authentic with yourself and your customers. When it comes to building a brand, honesty is the best policy. In the food business, your online success is heavily dependent on your offline performance, so always serve your customers right with great food and a rejuvenating ambiance.

Do not ever be in an illusion that digital marketing is something that anyone can do and try to do it yourself. It won't work and you will be simply wasting your time. Invest part of your budget in digital marketing and hire an expert to do it for you.

I as a food lover and digital marketer have seen great results with the implementation of digital marketing tactics in the food business. Being a food blogger who regularly blogs and vlogs on my Instagram Channel: GHOF, I feel food business has a lot to gain through social media and digital marketing. There are tremendous food outlets yet to tap into the power of digital media, and to wish to reach all of them through this book.

Author Biography

Nitish Mathur is a social media marketer and a passionate food blogger. He is presently managing a bootstrapped company; MindSync Media Pvt Ltd, which is a digital marketing firm based out of Bengaluru. Nitish is an avid food lover and food blogs at @GHOF on Instagram. During his free time, he loves to workout and plays badminton.

Where to Find Nitish
www.linkedin.com/in/nitmathur28
mindsyncindia.com

"I feel food business has a lot to gain through social media and digital marketing. There are tremendous food outlets yet to tap into the power of digital media and I wish to reach all of them through this book."

Resource
www.99dollarsocial.com/9-effective-strategies-for-restaurant-marketing

Backstage Secrets To Grow Your Business In The Music Industry

By Christian Fictoor

Are you a musician, an artist, in a band, a composer, a sound engineer or do you play any role in the world of music? Great, then this chapter is for you.

Have you ever thought, "I'm just one song away from success!"

A lot of us think that way when we begin and we very soon realize that things don't actually work that way. The music industry is about much more than composing great music. To succeed you need to have a real strategy, one that works alongside your artistic skills.

After you have written your song, after meticulously arranging the chord progressions, adding the right vocal pieces and producing your music, now the reality check begins.

Why Great Musicians Fail

- They produce great music, then spray and pray. They spray their music everywhere and pray that it works. Spraying and praying has a very high failure rate.
- Their path to success is not well thought out and they use one-off disconnected tactics.
- They think they can build a long music career on their own

when in reality they need a team, a decent network and the willingness to collaborate with a lot of people.

- They try to push their compositions onto record labels, promoters and publishers without actually trying to understand what these companies want, and identifying if you and they would work well together.

In today's world you just can't blame poor results on a lack of opportunities, as there are more ways to promote your music than ever before. It's all about having the right approach, understanding what works for you and how you can build on it.

I would like to take you through the stages that iGNITE! Music takes our musicians through to build and grow their businesses in the music industry.

Coone, The Hardstyle Pianist & David Spekter special act during the "Hard Bass 2018" event with over 25,000 people (photo credits: B2S).

As an example, one of our clients Jisk (pronounced Yisk), known as *The Hardstyle Pianist,* is a classically trained pianist from the Netherlands. In only two years, he managed to grow from posting acoustic versions of Hardstyle hit songs on YouTube, with a few hundred followers, to a sought after musician who plays at the biggest Hardstyle Events in Europe such as Hard Bass and Defqon.1.

Stage 1 – Getting to Know Your 'Scene'

To grow your music business, you'll need to grow a solid fan base. Selling your album to a few people isn't going to earn you a living. You'll need to cater to a larger audience while ensuring sustainable growth.

The only way you can succeed in growing your fan base is to really know your target audience; knowing *your scene'*, as it's referred to in the music industry. This might sound easy and too obvious but this is what most people skip, as they tend to jump to the next steps too soon, and then fail.

The term 'authenticity' is used as a buzzword but it's actually a very powerful strategy to use when growing your business, especially in the music industry. The reason is simple; sincerity comes through when you engage with your audience, they tend to trust you sooner and are more open to try your work.

In Jisk's case, he picked a scene that was close to his heart. As a teenager he visited several dance events and knew people in the scene. He understood the tone of voice, the look, the trends and the common topics people in the scene talk about.

Stage 2 – Becoming Part of 'Your Scene'

When you identify the scene that fits you and what you offer, the next step is becoming part of the scene. Please don't announce to your audience right away, "Hey I am <enter your name here> and I'm here to sell <your offer>." No!

Engage with these people on social media and other relevant online platforms by joining conversations about popular topics and voicing your opinion. It's important you realize that it's better to give something of value to your community first, before selling your product right away.

For a more personal relationship, it's preferable to use your personal social media accounts for this, not your fan page accounts. Get out and engage with your scene in real life, go to events where the people in your scene meet. Talk to them, learn from them, ask them what they think is hot and what's cold.

Make sure you are making notes of the feedback and input you receive, and build a solid understanding of what's going on in your scene, who the leading players are, who's losing ground, and the basic numbers in terms of market potential.

The key factor is to find that one thing which resonates with the people in your scene on an emotional level. In the Hardstyle scene, which is a subculture genre of the Dance Music genre, people feel strongly that they're part of a tight and respecting community; they call it their 'Hardstyle Family'. This is a perfect example of something that resonates on an emotional level.

Now that you have a fair understanding of your scene let's get ready to build your fanbase.

Stage 3 – Building Your Fanbase

Jisk knew there were already several famous acts in the Hardstyle scene, which was good because it showed there was a proven market. We also understood that in order for Jisk to stand out in his scene, he had to bring something unique to his audience. Jisk was also very particular about wanting to connect with his fans on an emotional level.

Combining his classical piano skills and his own love for the music genre he started to post YouTube videos under his artist name, 'Hardstyle Pianist', where he displayed his own musical arrangements of famous Hardstyle hits.

"The key factor is to find that one thing which resonates with the people in your scene on an emotional level." #TheGrowthHackingBook #GrowthHackingMovement #GrowthHackingDay

Jisk didn't stop there. He went on to tag the original artists of those hits. Over time, some of those artists began sharing his version on their social channels. As his YouTube channel started to gain traction, he added a Facebook page, an Instagram account and a website, to build a concrete online presence. What's important here is that he really engages with his audience and doesn't use social media as a one-way communication channel to broadcast music.

Every time he posts a video, it's like he's giving his audience a gift. Sometimes he asks them which song he should cover next.

People in his scene appreciate his original mix of classical music arrangements, and he is now very popular and well known to people in his scene.

Jisk was invited by Q-Dance, the leading worldwide Hardstyle event organizer, to play his first performance during the 'Freaqshow' event on New Year's Eve of 2016-2017.

Jisk knew that to grow his fan base further and turn his fans into lifetime customers, he had to go beyond just recording videos and taking up sporadic gigs at events. He had to scale up.

Given the combination of his knowledge of his scene, the online metrics he collected and our music marketing experience and expertise, we began working on building his recognizable and sustainable image. More importantly, we constantly used feedback from his ever-growing fanbase to tweak and fine tune his messaging and outreach.

Stage 4 – Selling, Scaling and the Patience Game

Let's discuss in detail, the ways artists generate revenue. This is the stage where you take your show on the road, grow your fanbase, sell tickets and increase the frequency of your new music releases. To do this you need to test your creative ideas, validate them and team up with the right people.

Main Sources of Revenue
- Ticket sales
- Music streaming
- Rights earned with airplay and live performances
- Merchandise sales
- Being a sponsored artist and influencer

Don't try to push the market or fans too much. Make them want you and love what you do, and they are more likely to become loyal fans. This is the stage where you need a lot of persistence, patience and perseverance as well as a great team.

You need to identify and partner with people from your existing audience, professionals from the music industry and experts who will voice their opinions and give feedback on your new releases, live shows and tour ideas.

Every element in your show, from the music, to the sound, lights and video, and to other show elements like clothing and special effects, need to come together to ensure that fans can relate and are touched on an emotional level. This will make your act an integral part of the scene forever.

Action Steps
- Pitch your general ideas, elevator pitch style.
- Brainstorm informally with your team and partners and value their input.

- Get input on rehearsals and possible tweaks to your performance.
- Get input for conceptualizing and designing your shows.
- Contact all relevant media channels and start cross-selling within your budget.
- After designing your show, organize a few closed events. Invite a select group of trusted people from your scene. Collect their feedback and use this information to tweak your show and ensure it's ready to tour.

Stage 5 – Keep That Buzz Going, Never Sit Back and Relax

Once you get a few shows right, you'll get more invitations and requests to perform and collaborate with established professionals in your scene.

Never take your audience for granted; you'll need to constantly innovate and stay relevant if you want a long sustainable career as a musician. Always be introducing new and original show elements and release interesting music to make sure people keep coming back to you.

Be talking to people in the scene to make sure you know what your audience wants, and you don't become a one-hit wonder.

There's no status quo. You either innovate and grow or decline. Growth is a continuous process and you can't ever afford to sit back and relax.

Lastly, if you're an artist and you want to grow your business, feel free to get in touch. I'll be more than happy to help you!

AUTHOR BIOGRAPHY

Christian Fictoor is the co-founder of iGNITE! Music B.V. and has worked as a Marketing Strategist and an Event Manager for organizations across Europe since 1996. He has an eagle eye when it comes to scouting and coaching artists, like the Hardstyle Pianist, who have gone on to become household names in their respective scenes.

Christian is known for his out-of-the-box thinking and energetic ways of working. He is an active member of the startup ecosystem and is part of the Google for Entrepreneurs initiative "Startup Weekend" in Enschede.

Christian has been a sounding board for startups in APAC and Europe. He's sought after by columnists and authors for opinions and advice, and has collaborated with Yaagneshwaran Ganesh on his books, *"Is Your Marketing in Sync or Sinking?"* and *"Syncfluence"*.

Where to Find Christian
www.linkedin.com/in/fictoorchristian

"There's no status quo. You either innovate and grow or decline. Growth is a continuous process. You can't ever afford to sit back and relax."

GROWING YOUR BRICK AND MORTAR BUSINESS IN THE DIGITAL ERA

By Priya Kalra

In this day and age where everything is available online, brick and mortar businesses are finding it very challenging to stay afloat. Companies like Amazon are taking over the product industry, making it easy for people to sit on their couch and order things to be delivered right to their doorstep. If large companies like Toys R Us are shutting down, why are small businesses still opening up and how are they growing?

My experience as a successful small business owner taught me that being involved in my local community and strategically using social media are the best and fastest ways to grow.

Strategies to Help Your Business Grow

Gain The Goodwill of Your Community

When you're the go-to person in your community, word of mouth referral is the best compliment your business can receive. Great reviews and referrals by others are quick ways to get more foot traffic into your store.

Empowering Other Business Owners

As a business owner, I was curious how other women balance their business and home lives. Running a business has its own set of challenges and trying to be the best version of you at home and in the professional world is a struggle many women go through.

I decided to interview women in business and share their stories on social media. Finding common ground and using the power of Facebook helped me to increase my fan base while supporting other small businesses.

Create Meaningful Relationships with Networking

Business owners often forget to work on their business, and not always in their business. Going out to network and meet people helps to develop long lasting relationships. When meeting people face to face, finding things in common to talk about is a good way to 'break the ice' and get an interesting conversation going.

"Brick and mortar businesses grow when they put the needs of their community first." #TheGrowthHackingBook #GrowthHackingMovement #GrowthHackingDay

Case study: Sponsoring a Community Event

Objective

Bringing the community together through a community event to raise awareness about my business.

The Event

I really wanted to throw an event that would bring the whole community together. I decided to put together a Children's Business Fair. Children were required to come up with a business idea and sell their products to the public. The kids set up their own booths, talked to the public and sold their products. They also had the responsibility of marketing the event and inviting their family and friends to come and support them.

Making it Special

I invited community influencers including the Mayor and city council members to be judges and hand out prizes to the top three winners.
I also asked local businesses to sponsor the event by donating raffle prizes, which helped spread the word about their businesses as well.

Results

We had an amazing turnout. Everyone who attended couldn't stop talking about how much fun they had and how much they are looking forward to the next event.

Growth Hacking Lesson

People who had never heard about my business became customers. I was able to connect with families and we talked about our common interests, which are helping our kids learn the value of money and seeing them experience entrepreneurship.

Brick and mortar businesses are always going to be here because face-to-face interaction is still valued, especially in the service industry. In today's digital age, reaching out to the public is much easier by using social media platforms in the right way, by paying attention to detail and by being actively involved in your community.

AUTHOR BIOGRAPHY

Priya Kalra is a global entrepreneur, mother, wife and cancer survivor. Currently Owner of Experimac Chandler in Arizona,USA, she has just launched her own CBD product business. With businesses in USA and another in Africa, she has a lot on her plate.

Raised in a tight-knit community in Zambia, Priya feels everyone she meets has influenced her life, but her mother is the author of her lifelong mantra, "Everything happens for a reason." Her quest for answers inspired Priya's *'Female Friday'* social media video series, where she interviews women entrepreneurs to explore why they started their businesses. "You never know whose story may help another woman take that step," she says. She is now interviewing Breast Cancer survivors to highlight how they conquered cancer.

Where to Find Priya
www.priyakal.com

"Be the go-to person for your industry, in your community."

GROWTH HACKING THE NEWSJACKING WAY

By Srish Agrawal

Without a flicker of doubt, we can term the last few years as *'The Period of Disruptive Transformation'*. Startups across the globe, with their unique business models and marketing ideas, have been able to ink unprecedented growth and success. They've gone from nowhere to enormous reach in a short span, now with billions of users worldwide. This was never imagined a few decades back.

Uber, Airbnb and others have shown the world how to carve out a niche and make a mark through creative, innovative and technical marketing strategies. They understand and believe in the latent potential of their products and services and work and execute well to transform this potential into reality.

The absolute focus on driving growth by new businesses has brought about a radical transformation, giving rise to a number of methods, tools and best practices that are aligned with consumer's lifestyle, behavioral psychology and real-time needs mapping. This simply didn't exist in traditional marketing.

The defining features of these growth hacking techniques have been their low-cost and surprising efficacy, allowing even the smallest startup to dream big and do big.

Newsjacking is one such viral marketing technique that I firmly believe can help startups multiply reach and amplify growth.

Riding your campaign on a wave of a news story that's all set up to spread like wildfire is the Art of Newsjacking. News stories tend to capture the attention of larger audiences more effectively than advertising, which makes Newsjacking a smart move that gets your marketing message across almost instantly and inexpensively.

Newsjacking is now an established expertise, which appears to be simple on the surface, however it requires considerable thought and expertise. In this short chapter, we introduce you to Newsjacking, show how it helps hack your business growth, and what you need to do for it to work flawlessly.

Newsjacking is Backed by Trust and the Ability to Go Viral

Trust plays a strong role in the consumption of any kind of message and communication. Advertising and marketing messages tend to be received with much lower trust-levels than a breaking news story. Further, people who are naturally less inclined to trust people tend to disregard mainstream news stories, and prefer blogs, social media and alternative opinions.

In addition, there has been a rapid shift from relying on traditional print news to consuming news from online sources. As online news publishers tend to update developing stories continuously and many of these stories have the potential to go viral, marketers have a wealth of sources to engage in Newsjacking.

Sales and marketing professionals can piggyback on potentially viral news stories and design their marketing messages and campaigns around them. The primary objective is to create increased visibility and positive opinion about the brand they are committed to feature.

"Newsjacking helps improve SEO ranking, promotes thought leadership, increases conversion rates and enhances content marketing and social engagement." #TheGrowthHackingBook #GrowthHackingMovement #GrowthHackingDay

Use Newsjacking to Break Sales Records

There are a number of benefits associated with newsjacking:

SEO: Search engines promote content that appear first in news results. If you cover a news topic before others do, you could rank higher in the search results. Improved SEO results in improved sales figures.

Thought leadership: Helps you to position yourself as a thought leader in your area of expertise, if you provide detailed insights and observations on a developing news story related to your brand.

Boost conversion rates: Newsjacking can boost conversion rates dramatically by directing traffic to your website and by enhancing your credibility and marketing success.

Improve content marketing: Newsjacking provides raw material for your content marketing funnel, helping you ride on viral news stories to remain relevant.

Improve social media engagement: Provides a great opportunity to engage your audience and make an impact on their lives by discussing what matters to them.

Four Stages of a News Story

While most savvy businesses have already begun to engage in some form of Newsjacking via social media, it's important to understand the normal news cycle before trying Newsjacking.

Stage 1: An event takes place and the news is broken.

Stage 2: There's a general scramble for information as journalists seek more information to report.

Stage 3: The news story peaks and begins to plateau.

Stage 4: The story becomes old and no longer appeals to the audience.

How to Successfully Implement Newsjacking

It's difficult for an overstretched content marketing team to remain updated about the latest news headlines, but with a few simple tricks and a little effort, even a small team can Newsjack successfully.

1. **RSS Alerts:** Set up RSS alerts about topics that interest your readers and subscribe to topics that are of particular importance to your industry. Do not limit yourself to industry news, Newsjacking requires you to use news headlines that impact your target audience so use their behavioral and psychographic indices and subscribe to customized alerts.

2. **Social Media:** Monitor social media to understand what your followers are talking about. Social media monitoring tools such as Hubspot can be particularly helpful to critically evaluate topics of interest for your followers. Build a campaign based on which topic is being discussed by your audience on social media.

3. **Keyword Search Volume:** Use keyword search volume, then build content based on a topic that you have decided to Newsjack. Google Trends and Google Keyword Planner are effective tools to help you focus on a topic that interests your audience. You can also research long tail keywords and implement them in your

SEO efforts to positively influence the SERPs when you have comparatively shorter deadlines.

4. **Know The Topic:** Read extensively about the topic you have chosen to write about, especially if you plan to write a blog post. Verify your sources and cross-check with secondary sources of the news story. If you plan to use a developing news story as part of a social media strategy, make sure to be factually correct.

5. **Be Quick and Accurate:** While it is important to write quickly, before the news story becomes common knowledge, it is also important to write accurately. Don't be too choosy about your photographs and formatting, as these actions can delay publishing.

6. **Use The Tools:** Use the right tools to get your message across. Don't restrict yourself to textual social media and blog content. Integrate videos and infographics into your posts, as they have a higher chance of going viral than written content.

7. **Introduce Your Angle:** The reason why businesses engage in Newsjacking is to communicate their existence, relevance and thought leadership. Introduce your own angle to the story, and make sure to differentiate your content from others who have already written on the topic.

8. **Use Public Relations:** Do not stop at social media and your own blogs to market Newsjacking items. Instead, contact reputed Journalists and Public Relations Agencies, especially if you have information about something that they still don't. This can prove to be an opportunity for you to be cited by credible sources, enhancing your image.

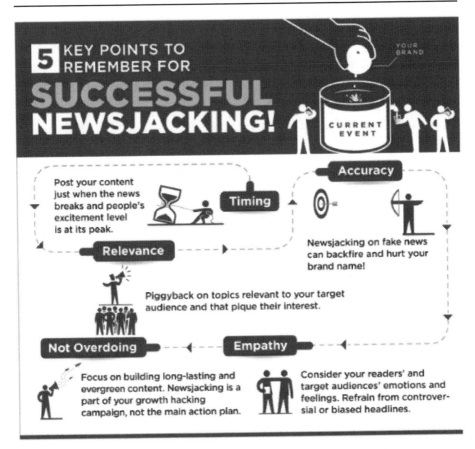

Newsjack with Caution - Five Points to Remember

It's important to exercise caution while Newsjacking. Graham C.L. Davey, Ph.D., the author of, *'Why We Worry'*, wrote on *Psychology Today* that news bulletins can have a negative impact on people if the content isn't pleasant. This is why marketers should be careful to avoid news stories that may evoke negative emotions such as fear, disgust, contempt or even skepticism. For instance, an earthquake is certainly not the situation to capitalize on. The negative emotions that consumers experience from such a tragic event, may get projected onto your brand.

To make sure your Newsjacking efforts are successful, it is important to consider the following five points carefully:

   1. Timing: Make sure you launch a social media and blogging campaign just when the news breaks and Journalists are still scrambling to find additional information. It's at this point that people's excitement level intensifies. Once journalists begin writing detailed opinion pieces, you're unlikely to benefit from Newsjacking as the news agencies normally do a better job at reporting than marketing agencies ever will.

Example: Oreo's real-time Newsjacking effort during a 35-minute blackout earned it accolades and sales. It was witty, potentially viral and non-offensive.

2. **Relevance:** Choose the news topic you are going to piggyback on very carefully. The news story should be relevant to your business or at least to your target audience. Use demographic and psychographic indices to discover which news trends will interest your readers the most. Choose only the most relevant topics to kick start your Newsjacking campaign.

    Example: "This storm blows (but free shipping doesn't)! Today only!", screamed Urban Outfitters, leading to criticisms for being irrelevant. The company experienced brand cancellations after their Newsjacking attempt failed.

3. **Accuracy:** With fake news becoming a global problem, people are increasingly wary about what they read online. Carefully verify everything you write and crosscheck with at least two reputed news agencies before engaging in Newsjacking. Trying to push a marketing message via news that's not credible can hurt your brand more than it can ever help.

    Example: Krispy Kreme's *Tastiest Eclipse in History*, campaign was successful because it provided accurate information about an eclipse while also promoting Krispy Kreme Donuts, suggesting they should be eaten when dark.

4. **Empathy:** As discussed previously, consider your readers' and target audiences' emotions and feelings. Avoid negative news headlines and don't use stories that may evoke skepticism among readers. Choose neutral and positive news stories in order to make an impact on your readers' emotions. For instance, while

warning about impending summer heat can be construed as empathic, the same cannot be said of an actual heat wave that has resulted in a large number of casualties.

Example: In the middle of the Syrian conflict, fashion designer Kenneth Cole tweeted *'boots on the ground'*, in a cringe-worthy attempt to Newsjack that failed.

5. **Not overdoing:** The key to Newsjacking is to not overdo it. The more you rely on breaking news to support your growth hacking campaign, the less likely your original content is going to be impactful. Focus on building long-lasting and evergreen content that isn't newsy. This will help your SEO and marketing and will solidify your status as a thought leader. Newsjacking can be a small part of your content marketing strategy, not the main action plan.

Example: In India, dairy company Amul, successfully engages in Newsjacking despite overdoing it, and is widely popular for its timely and relevant socio-political cartoons in print media. This doesn't work for most brands.

Before Newsjacking a Developing Story:

- Can our audience take offense if we jack this news story?
- Will we be able to align our core brand values with this story?
- How will a complete stranger react to our content on this news story?
- Does it look like we are trying too hard or that we are out of touch?
- Are we exploiting a situation to our benefit?

Only use newsjacking to show your readers that you're aware of what impacts them and that you're in touch with stories that affect them on a regular basis, without neglecting your own content marketing strategy.

Key Points to Remember

- Newsjacking is an effective content strategy to enhance sales and marketing efforts.

- Newsjacking involves choosing a news topic that will help your brand to connect with your audience and promote you as a thought leader.

- Newsjacking presents your brand as being aware of what's happening in your target audience's lives.

- Newsjacking helps improve SEO ranking, promotes thought leadership, increases conversion rates and enhances content marketing and social engagement.

How to Newsjack

- Choose the right moment to capitalize on a news story and remain alert to new developments.

- Set up RSS alerts, monitor social media for trends, and engage in keyword research for finalizing news topics.

- Read extensively about the chosen topic and write informed posts that are not problematic.

- Focus on accuracy of facts and don't offend your target audience.

- Promote your Newsjacked content to your audience with a positive sense of humor, a bit of sarcasm and enough empathy to connect with them rationally and emotionally.

- Display empathy towards your audience and for those involved in the actual news.

- Most importantly, make sure that you have a wide content marketing strategy and do not depend on Newsjacking alone to create content.

Stay updated and focus on new trends and technologies to stay relevant with your marketing efforts. AI-Artificial Intelligence, Machine learning, AR-Augmented Reality and VR-Virtual Reality and other technologies are redefining the growth hack game at lightning pace. Gear up to weave them into your marketing and carve your way to success and growth.

Happy Growth Hacking!

AUTHOR BIOGRAPHY

Srish Agrawal is a Corporate Branding and Internet Marketing Strategist, Angel Investor, Speaker, Founder and CEO at A1 Future Technologies.

A veteran in the branding & Internet marketing ecosystem, Srish is the founder of multiple successful online businesses. Riding the wave from the dot-com era he built a remarkable company generating 100 percent of its revenues through online marketing. His client base, routed entirely from the overseas market, was acquired without him setting foot across the waters.

Srish's in-depth knowledge of branding and marketing coupled with his unparalleled experience and ability to keep up with industry dynamics has been a significant growth driver for him and all those he has consulted.

Srish has been recognized as one of the Top 100 Digital Marketing Experts by various online publications for his prolific achievements.

Where to Find Srish
www.linkedin.com/in/srishagrawal
www.srish.com
www.A1future.com

Google: "Help a Reporter Out"

How To Brand Leverage Offline Marketing For Audience Growth

By S. Shiva SriCharan

Companies focus on creating awareness, brand building and engagement through digital and social media platforms, to reach their target audience and provide them with products and services.

Now I ask you, what's the point in targeting an audience in the digital world and ignoring them in the real world? Whether companies are selling products, software like apps or services, having the right approach to your customer is critical.

In the history of business, companies with great products have failed in the market. There are many reasons why but it iterates that the customer is the most important person who companies can't ignore.

We cannot push products and services into the market and become unicorns overnight. The right approach is to understand what customers need and know their pain points well; only then do you offer products and services. This approach will focus your marketing efforts and ensure long-term engagement with your customers.

Businesses who deliver personalized and unique experiences, ones that compliment their products and services, win the audience game.

To build deeper relationships with customers, companies need to do more than just sell. Companies need to influence others, make referrals and work strategically to bring new products to the market. Customer engagement is imperative and a strategic approach to thoroughly understand their buying journeys and incorporate this information into advertising, marketing and the creation of products and services.

In this digital age, offline marketing is one of the most powerful tools you can take advantage of. When the world is going digital and future technologies like artificial intelligence, machine learning, deep learning, block chain and connected devices have become the norms in business, how can offline mediums like television, print, radio and cinema still hold relevance?

Indian ADEX estimated to grow at 14% in 2019. The fastest Growing Ad market in the world

groupᵐ

Medium	Ad spend (INR crs)					
	2014	2015	2016	2017	2018f	2019f
TV	19,411	23,022	25,350	27,961	33,577	38,612
Print	16,108	16,800	17,472	17,779	17,970	18,368
Digital	3,402	4,950	7,300	9,490	12,337	16,038
Outdoor	2,483	2,582	2,750	2,942	3,202	3,536
Radio	1,808	1,997	2,240	2,419	2,709	3,116
Cinema	340	408	560	672	806	1,008
All media	43,552	49,758	55,671	61,263	70,602	80,678

Take a closer look at the statistics in the report, *'This Year Next Year 2019 India'*, released by Group M the world's largest media investment company. Group M is owned by the world's largest media conglomerate, WPP.

As per the report, Indian advertising expenditure is estimated to grow at 14% in 2019, which makes it the fastest growing Ad market in the world. Digital advertising is the major contributor for growth and traditional media like Television and Print still dominates the market. Approximately 70% of the ad spend in India is driven by television and print media together and 19% goes to digital ad spend.

This reiterates the importance of traditional and offline medium as one of the most powerful tools in our digital age.

How Does Offline Media Help Brands?

Unlike digital engagement, which happens through social media posts, videos, podcasts, downloadable e-books and whitepapers for example, offline engagement is quite different; a mixture of both traditional and offline marketing solutions.

Traditional media and offline media helps you find an audience in the real world, who might be interested in your products and services.

Traditional media like television, print, radio and cinema helps send a brand message to a massive market. Offline media helps to find prospective buyers who engage with your brand's products and services.

Offline engagement can help businesses connect with prospects who might be interested in products and services.

Types of Offline Engagement:

- Events
- Activations
- Demos
- Kiosks
- Hoardings
- Radio ads
- Digital OOH
- Cinema Advertising
- Retail
- Transit Media
- Rural advertising
- Mobile van branding

In this world of distractions and noise, people tend to be on the move constantly. This gives brands an added opportunity to grab attention. A key study reveals that our attention span time today is just over six seconds.

Offline media has taken a back seat due to its lack of accountability, unlike digital media where accountability is transparent. Over the years, companies have found offline media difficult to deal with and have moved towards investing heavily in digital media.

"Businesses who deliver personalized and unique experiences, ones that compliment their products and services, win the audience game." #TheGrowthHackingBook #GrowthHackingMovement #GrowthHackingDay

Media Disruption Solution

Disruption is the key and it is happening everywhere.

Television has been disrupted through stand-alone OTT (Over-The-Top) streaming media platforms on websites and apps, which can be accessed on personal computers, smartphones and tablets, as well as integrated smart TVs.

Radio has been disrupted through online digital radio and community radio.

Print has been disrupted through digital print editions and ebooks.

Cinema has been disrupted through digital programming solutions from Qube, UFO and CiniCloud, Amazon Prime and Zee 5 for example.

Outdoor media has been disrupted with the digital OOH solution providers like Posterscope and Adonmo, on taxi advertising in India.

Events have been disrupted with LinkedIn Events and through ticketing platforms like MeraEvents, BookMyShow, Eventbrite and Townscript, for example.

Online-to-offline and offline-to-online engagement is a new challenge for businesses to explore, as you don't want to miss customers on either of these platforms.

For example, LinkedIn used their latest campaign *#inittogether* in 2019, to bring professionals from different backgrounds onto the platform through online and offline media. They have used outdoor, print, television and airport branding very effectively in all their major markets around the world.

Spotify launched in India in February 2019 and raised awareness through offline media like print, in outdoor bus shelters, foot bridges, taxis and mall branding, to showcase its 40 million song databases and get subscribers to sign-up for the music streaming service.

A decade ago, a major brand like Unilever would take nine out of 10 television advertisements on all the leading broadcasting networks across the entire nation of India. Today the scenario is quite different with emerging technology companies taking the spotlight on every major offline medium.

Over the last five years, companies have spent heavily on offline mediums including television, outdoor and print; due to the emergence of ecommerce and technology based companies like Flipkart, Amazon India, Google, Netflix, Zee5, Swiggy, Uber Eats and Zomato.

The Opportunities

It is difficult to find a person without a mobile phone. India is the fastest growing market in mobile and data consumption with 627 million Internet users and 1.1 billion mobile devices.

In the age of Netflix, social media, TikTok and PubG, how does a brand attract its customer?

Digital media and engagement gives brands an opportunity to know their customers through social media interactions, app downloads and usage, and data analytics.

We know our prospects are in the real world so how does a brand reach out to them?

A prospect can be anywhere:

- On the road
- In a shopping mall or coffee shop
- In a multiplex
- At theme parks
- In a restaurant
- Sitting at home
- At school or college
- At a workplace

Offline media helps to grab attention with:

- A television commercial
- A radio jingle
- An advertisement played on a big screen
- Billboards and hoardings
- Taxi advertising
- Retail branding
- Metro rail branding
- Community events
- A product demo in a mall

The Numbers Game for Marketers

Television: TV advertising grew to 14% in 2018 to reach Rs. 305 billion. The number of private satellite channels increased to 885.

Print: Print advertising stood at 29% to reach Rs. 217 billion in 2018.

Radio: Radio grew by 7.5% in 2018 to reach Rs. 31.3 billion. There are a total of 386 radio stations in India.

Digital Media: At 42%, digital media grew to reach Rs. 169 billion in 2018. Broadband subscribers increased to 512 million and rural Internet users grew to reach 197 million. Smartphone users number 340 million and Integrated Smart TVs crossed 10 million users. Digital ad spends grew 34% to Rs. 154 billion. Digital subscriptions grew 262% to reach Rs. 14 billion in 2018.

Out of Home (OOH): OOH media grew by 8.8% with a reach of Rs 37.3 billion in 2018. Out of this, Rs. 1.5 billion is generated by the Digital OOH (DOOH), in the same year. About 70,000+ digital displays are in airports, metro and railway stations and malls.

Events: The organized events and activation segment grew to 15.6% in 2018 to reach Rs. 75 billion. Ticket sales contributed to more than Rs. 7 billion and digital events and activations grew by over 35%.

Cinema: In-cinema advertising grew 17% to Rs. 7.5 billion in 2018. There are 9,601 total screens in India out of which 6,651 are single screens and 2,950 are multiplex screens in India.

Source: *'A billion screens of Opportunity – Indian Media & Entertainment sector – March 2019',* by FICCI and EY.

Conclusion

Offline engagement drives lead generation, brand awareness and business building challenges in the real world and the online world. As technology evolves, so does the industry. In coming years, we can hope to see a level playing field where both offline and online marketing strategies are used.

As existing markets mature, the advancement in technology adaptation allows us to see greater innovations with unique concepts in the marketing domain from new age marketers, technology enthusiasts and start-ups and entrepreneurs who focus on engaging with their customers.

Understand where your customers are, what they do and what they need from you. Plan your marketing and advertising with this information in mind.

Don't be like so many other companies who waste huge amounts of money on advertising because they didn't take the time to find out exactly who their customers are and what they want. This is how they lose the game.

Offline and online engagement must strike a balance between the customer and a relevant, engaging strategy. With proper execution and great team support, companies can create magic and capture their market.

AUTHOR BIOGRAPHY

Mr. S. Shiva SriCharan is an experienced marketer with 13+ years expertise in media, branding and customer experience.

He has worked with the best brands in India such as Unilever, Coca Cola, Pepsi, Samsung, Airtel, BSNL, ICICI Prudential, JCB among others. He has executed more than 1000+ campaigns in South India markets (Telangana and Andhra Pradesh) in cinema, outdoor, radio, print and rural mediums.

He has worked with leading agencies Group M, MindShare, Ogilvy, BBDO.

Shiva is currently working with startups in Dairy, Construction, Adtech and Edtech markets.

Shiva is the founder of FameBoat Media - helping businesses grow with marketing and technology solutions.

Where to Find Shiva
www.linkedin.com/in/shivasricharan

"Understand where your customers are and what they need from you and plan your advertising and marketing accordingly."

Online Success Secrets
For Health And Wellness Practitioners,
Coaches And Consultants

By Lisa Robbins

———◆———

Are you working too many hours, stressing over clients who don't fit your vision of ideal, trading your time for money and not being paid what you are worth?

It's painful and stressful wondering where your next client will come from and not knowing if you'll manage to create enough income to pay for what you and your family need next month.

If you've been relying on referrals up until now, charging by the hour for your services, and trying to solve every problem your clients have, you will face burn out big time, if you haven't already.

If you long for a consistent flow of leads that are right for your business, leads that will turn into clients who truly appreciate you and want to pay you for helping them, you need to know that this is completely possible.

Wouldn't it be perfect to have an automated marketing system that brings a consistent flow of prequalified clients, right onto your calendar? People who actually want to work with you and pay you well for your help? That would be beautiful.

Imagine your new clients taking a quick jaunt through your marketing funnel, adding themselves to your appointment calendar and giving you all the information you need to know about them, before you even get on the phone with them. Sounds awesome, yes?

This would mean you could book the vacation you've wanted to take for so long. Epic.

You could pay your debts and stop paying interest to debtors. That's beautiful too.

You could call your own shots, look after your family and leave a legacy for them. You could pay your child's student loans, pay your parents' mortgage or buy tiny homes for homeless people, whatever you fancy.

What Happens In Growth Hacking Book, Stays in Growth Hacking Book

It happened to me. I wasn't in my passion zone and was working with companies whose products, services and industries; I had absolutely no interest in.

I wasn't planning or strategizing and felt like I was going from busy to busier. I actually was busier all the time: learning more, doing more and becoming more overwhelmed by the day.

I didn't have a consistent marketing system to bring a steady flow of prequalified leads directly to me.

I wasn't specializing with one type of client and was burning myself out doing everything for every type of client.

Speaking of burnout, being the CEO of your business is one thing, being the Marketing Manager is another, being the SEO Expert, the Health and Wellness Coach, the Website Builder, the Copywriter, the Accountant and every other role, is something out of this world.

Don't be and do everything. Pare down every single aspect of your business to be strategic, simple and profitable. Do only what you need to do and hire out the rest.

"Don't be and do everything. Pare down every single aspect of your business to be strategic, simple and profitable. Do only what you need to do and hire out the rest." #TheGrowthHackingBook #GrowthHackingMovement #GrowthHackingDay

The 4-Key Success Strategy

1. **Focus on Simple and Profitable** — Identify the top three critical steps you must take to move your business forward right now. Follow these steps to a tee, and do not add anything else to your list until all three are complete. Only then can you add three more. No more overwhelm, only strategic, focused results.

   Action Step 1: Create a CRITICAL TOP THREE LIST

   To help you determine what is critical and what is not, do a brain dump of everything you need and want to do for your business. Once you've completed your list, identify the top three critical items on your list that will help your business move forward right now and place them on their own list.

   Attach your *Critical Top Three List* to a place where you can always see it while working. This is your daily guide, do not stray from taking care of the items on your list and do not be distracted by anything NOT on your CRITICAL TOP THREE LIST.

2. **Offer a Specific Result for a Specific Client with a Specific Problem** — Specialize in what you know best, what you are passionate about and what you have the most experience with. Helping every client with any problem, will cause you to crash and burn fast.

Pick one specific client to serve, with a specific problem, and focus on this issue in all of your copywriting and marketing. Talk to one client only; copywriting that speaks to multiple types of clients with different problems is immediately confusing to you and your potential clients.

For example, specialize in weight loss, healthy aging, nutrition for mental health, restore harmony to your energy field, balance hormones, improve range of motion, or stress reduction, etc. Choose only one problem.

Focus on the one big problem your ideal client has, the one they are motivated and willing to pay you to help them solve. If a client does not have this exact problem, they are not your ideal client and you are better off, not being distracted by this, and instead referring them to a colleague who *does* specialize in their problem.

Action Step 2: Answer the following three questions

1. Who is your ideal client?

2. What one big problem do they have that you are able to help them with?

3. What one result will you offer to help them achieve this result?

3) **Automate Your Marketing Funnel** — Create an automated marketing funnel that has your ideal clients reaching out to you and asking for your help.

In a world of automation, why wouldn't you automate your marketing and sales to the largest degree possible?

An automated marketing funnel can:

a) Filter out people who are not a proper fit with you and what you offer.

b) Attract your ideal clients, who follow this model:

   1. They fit with the type of client you serve,

   2. They have the one big problem you help with,

   3. They desire the result you can help them attain.

c) Have them book an appointment with you on your own calendar, on any days that you choose to work.

d) Have them give you all the information you need about their business and themselves, before deciding to work with them.

e) Raise your credibility by showing that your business is based around genuinely caring for them, by first providing value in helping them solve their big problem.

Action Step 3: Start Your Marketing Funnel by Creating a Lead Magnet that truly helps your client:

   1. List the steps your client needs to take to solve their big problem.

   2. Create a report, video or audio that helps your client solve one of those steps.

   3. Offer this 'lead magnet' on your website in exchange for their email address.

4) **Turn on Traffic** — Send a steady flow of traffic to your funnel, and pump it up whenever you need to increase the flow of new clients and sales.

Traffic can come from many sources, including:

Organic Search: A long term and very effective approach to improving your online presence so people can find you through their searches.

Social Media: A medium term approach to building a following over time, which can be accelerated with the amount of effort spent. Social Media offers an excellent testing ground for your Marketing Funnel before you move to Paid Advertising.

Paid Advertising: A quick approach to sending targeted traffic directly to your offer. Paid advertising is best when started based on organic results, started small, then monitored and tweaked for effectiveness. Once confident in your results, you can scale up, paying for more ads that send more targeted buyers to your offer.

Guest Posts: A long term approach to improving the exposure of your products and services to your ideal clients, sending leads back to your offers, and improving your backlink score on search engines, which is an established criteria for ranking your website.

Directories and Listings: A short to medium term approach to improving the ranking score of your website on search engines. If you want to show up high on Google searches, then one of your first steps will be to optimize your Google My Business and Google Maps listings.

Collaborative Projects: A long-term approach to improving your exposure to ideal clients around the world. This book is an excellent example of a collaborative approach, where authors contribute value by teaching about their specialty in a chapter. Authors may each share links to purchasing this book with their audiences. One author's teaching may attract the attention of a member of another author's audience. That person may want to know more about how the author can help them and become a client.

Action Step 4: Optimize your *Google My Business* Listing

For instructions go to: www.MapleKeyDigital.ca/optimize-my-google-my-business-listing/

AUTHOR BIOGRAPHY

Lisa Robbins is an Online Marketing Strategist who specializes in helping Health and Wellness Practitioners, Coaches and Consultants create an effective and profitable automated online presence. Over the past 10 years, Lisa has helped start ups, authors, health and wellness practitioners and a variety of small local businesses to optimize and automate their online marketing.

Lisa is a Registered Holistic Nutritionist and has a B.Sc. in Holistic Nutrition. She is Founder of the video series *Incredible Healing Journals and* author of *The Cancer Journal: Heal Yourself.* Lisa has worked on collaborative book projects, including: *Cancer Cure and Survivor Stories, The Power of 100,* and *When You're Done Expecting: A Collection of Heartfelt Stories from Mothers All Across the Globe.*

Where to Find Lisa
www.MapleKeyDigital.ca

"Complete the four Action Steps above to be well on your way to automating your health and wellness business."

MINDSET

Learn how to navigate the
business ups and downs by
changing your mindset.

BEND THE REALITY OF NETWORKING

By Ruchi G. Kalra

"Hi, my name is (fill in the blank). I'm a (fill in the blank), I work for (fill in the blank)," and 30 seconds later everyone knows your elevator pitch.

Raise your hand if you've been to a networking event and every conversation starts like this. Keep your hand up if you've ever caught yourself rehearsing your 30-second pitch while others are giving theirs? I'm sure quite a few hands stayed up. In fact, it's this type of meet and greet dance that most networking events start and end with. I believe is the real key to networking, is what happens in between, which is often overlooked.

Traditional Meet and Greet

Networking is so much more than our name tags, the companies we own or work for, what we do for them and pushing through those awkward interactions. It's a scary process for some but it really doesn't have to be. Many people cringe at the thought of talking to strangers and selling them on their business. These are the same people who heave a sigh of relief once their 30-second pitch is over.

Twist Your Networking Mindset

What can we do to change this mindset and bend the reality of networking? How do we get ourselves unshackled from those memorized 30-second pitches and find a way to get those palms to stop sweating?

We each have stories that define us so much more than a basic pitch. Everyone has a story and that story gets completely lost in a canned 30-second spiel. Authentic networking is a very simple concept and can be summarized in two words - Build Relationships!

I can tell you that relationships should be the one and only thing that should be on your mind when you walk into a networking event. We get so caught up in collecting connections and business cards that we forget the human aspect of these events. Think of these as friendships rather than connections. Work on getting to know another person's story. It's the one key concept that should be included in everything we say or do at these events.

Don't walk into these events thinking, "How can these people help me?" Walk in thinking the exact opposite, "I wonder who I can help today?"

Friends Like to Help Friends

Let's take a look at an everyday life example: your neighbor asks you for a referral, it could be for a social media guru, a plumber or contractor. Do you refer a friend that you know personally or someone you casually met at a networking event? Most of us would go with the first option and recommend a friend. Most people like to do business with people they trust, or at least know through their friends and connections.

"Authentic networking is a very simple concept and can be summarized in two words - Build Relationships!"
#TheGrowthHackingBook
#GrowthHackingMovement
#GrowthHackingDay

Find the Right Fit For You

A key component to building relationships is picking the right type and size of networking groups you want to be part of. Sometimes smaller is better, as it's easier to build meaningful relationships. Pick a group of people who have a similar mindset to yours. When you attend these events, remember you're taking time away from your business, so make it more than a business card exchange session. Get to know their stories, their passions and their reasons for building their dreams.

Hello Digital Networking

It's important to note that in recent years networking has morphed tremendously due to the Internet. The number of active online community groups has grown at an impressive rate. Digital communities have helped people and businesses create a new type of online presence and a very acceptable method of recommendations and referrals.

The best way of increasing your online relationships is to engage in the platform that best targets your interest group. For Facebook it may take the form of a few of your neighborhood communities, on LinkedIn it may be common interest groups and on Twitter it may be following the influencers who are connected with your industry. There are many other platforms like Snapchat, YouTube, Instagram and the video platform, TikTok.

An easy way to build your online relationships is to set aside a few minutes each day to engage with others within these online communities. Nurture relationships by commenting on people's posts, sending direct messages to contacts and browsing to get a feel of what's trending in a particular group or on a platform that day. These comments and posts will organically grow into relationships. Be genuine in your comments and posts, as it'll not only help you connect with people on social media, it will also help build organic networking relationships along the way. Use the power of social media to get in front of and stay in touch with people you wouldn't have met otherwise.

Do I Know You?

I can't tell you how many times I've introduced myself to people and upon hearing my name they have looked at me like they know me. After a further conversation, we realize we "know" each other from our neighborhood groups or through comments on mutual friend's pages on social media. You form an instant connection as you realize Ruchi is a good friend of your best friend Rachel. What comes next is a Facebook Friend request or an Instagram follow and a new relationship has started. Online relationships are a must for any company in the world today.

Don't use every social media platform out there because it will overwhelm you. Make sure you know when and where your target audience is most active and use those platforms.

Do's and Don'ts of Building Business Friendships and Changing the Way You Network:

Don'ts:

- Never walk into an event to sell your products and services.
- Look at people as opportunities and connections.
- Let the angst or desperation of wanting business show.
- Randomly send friend requests to people on any social media platform.
- Get caught up using every social media platform.

Do's:

- Make an effort to listen more than talk.
- Get away from the standard networking script.
- Work on remembering names from the first introduction. Get to know their story and the story behind their business.
- Be open to meeting anyone and everyone and see how you can be of value.
- Give a shout out to and support other business owners on social media.

Evaluate Your Goals and Values

There's no one-size-fits-all for networking. You need to ask yourself what networking means to you and what you want from it. There's no right or wrong way but an evaluation of your core values and principles will help guide your path to growing your relationship goals.

Redefine the networking equation
From: Meeting People + Making Connections = Networking.

To: Meaningful Relationships + Valued Connections = Business Growth.

Plant those seeds today for rewards tomorrow.

If there is one message you need to take away from this chapter, it's to focus on building relationships and friendships and business growth will follow.

Think of the networking process as planting seeds and you could see the results in as soon as a month or it could be two or three years down the road. Be genuine and open yourself up to others, connecting in an authentic way. You'll build relationships and deep meaningful friendships that will be with you for the rest of your life.

Always remember, "By working together we all rise higher".

AUTHOR BIOGRAPHY

Ruchi was born in India and moved to Africa when she was nine and has lived in the U.S. since she moved there for college in 1986. Her journey brought her to the U.S. at 15 years of age and she quickly realized that to live in the dorms, she had to learn to build friendships and relationships in an unknown world and she had to do it fast.

Ruchi has always been a people person and spent a lot of time connecting with people on a heart-to-heart level. When she ended up in the marketing world, her approach to networking didn't stray too far from her core being and values.

She has a Bachelor of Science in Math & Computer Science and an MBA in Marketing.

Over the years she's worked in various roles in Revenue Accounting, Sales Planning and Analysis, and Marketing.

Ruchi founded Dancing Raindrops Inc., a consulting and strategy firm to help small businesses to tell their stories to help grow their businesses.

Where to Find Ruchi
www.linkedin.com/in/ruchigkalra
www.dancingraindropsinc.com

"When you attend networking events, build relationships with the people you meet by learning their story."

Leveraging The Power Of Relationships To Grow Your Online Business

By Kelisha Mills

If you want to grow your business fast, you better get into the habit of growing your relationships. With the rise of social media and other forms of communication like conferencing, it's now easier than ever to reach out to people who have the same likes and interests as you.

When I started my business online, I was relatively unknown. I live in the Caribbean and although I was well travelled and started my entrepreneurial journey as a young woman, I had no exposure in the online business world. I would now call myself a legitimate, true entrepreneur, because my business has been my only source of income for the past twelve years. I took the financial risk, invested in myself, and my business, then failed miserably and succeeded greatly.

In 2014, I closed my business due to the economic downturn and due to some bad business decisions I had made in my most profitable years. After overcoming a bout of depression and not having any idea of what to do next, I decided to pair my education with my roller coaster entrepreneurial experience and started anew as a business coach.

There was one big challenge. I had NO audience. Business coaching was essentially unheard of in my part of the world and small business owners couldn't understand why they needed to pay someone to show them how to run their businesses. Within my first year, I grew my business to a sustainable level, went from being unknown to speaking at events, connected with and interviewed hundreds of women- all thanks to leveraging the power of relationships.

"If you want to grow your business fast, get into the habit of growing your relationships."#TheGrowthHackingBook #GrowthHackingMovement #GrowthHackingDay

I want to share with you how I was able to do this with my **GROW Method**. It's the formula I used to hack rapid growth in my coaching business. Follow this method for one month and watch your follower and subscriber numbers increase.

G: Get to know your tribe

You probably have heard the story of a young adopted girl who grew up in an environment totally alien to her. She longed to find someone who would understand and connect with her. She left no stones unturned, reached out to many and eventually found people who felt like family. They had the same likes, values and interests. They welcomed her with open arms and were embraced in return. This young girl had finally found her tribe.

As a business owner, you must also find your tribe. Your tribe or business network, are founders/entrepreneurs/owners who have the same values and goals as you. They speak the same language, have similar experiences and have overcome some of the same challenges as you. These are the people you want to connect with.

Helen Keller once said; *"Alone we can do so little; together we can do so much."* This is also true in business. When I began to collaborate with other women entrepreneurs, my authority, influence and reach grew so fast. I let go of the idea that I knew everything and that others in the same field were rivals. I began to embrace my tribe, and invited them to speak on my platforms. I became known for bringing women entrepreneurs in my country together. How amazing is that?

This can happen for you too. However, there's a correct way to reach out. Trying to connect with a tribe in the wrong way can get you expelled from their circles entirely. I want to share with you how I approach it.

I want you to write down your goal for the amount of followers or connections you want to have across all your platforms. For each platform, search for those who you believe have similar goals, interests and values. Start with those near your geographical location, and then spread out nationally and internationally.

Let's use a New York bridal florist as an example to find businesses to connect with using the following platforms:

- **Google:** Google keywords for your business, example: Flowers, florist, bridal florist in New York, New York bridal florist. Make a list of local bridal florists you'd like to connect with.

- **Facebook:** In the Facebook search bar, use the same keywords you used in your Google search. Also, look in tabs under All, Marketplace, Posts, People, Photos, Videos, Pages, Places, Groups, Apps, Events and Links. Make a list of businesses you'd like to connect with.

- **Instagram:** Search for keywords under Top, Accounts, Tags and Places. Make a list of businesses you'd like to connect with.

- **LinkedIn:** Search your network and their connections.

- **Twitter:** Search for hashtags, pages and people. Make a list of the businesses you'd like to connect with.

R: Reach Out

Using your list, start sending out friend requests, direct messages, and emails. Make sure you have at least one contact or group in common. Do your research and make sure this is someone you want in your tribe or network. Sometimes people can be skeptical about friend requests, messages and emails coming from people they don't know, so be prepared to be ignored or blocked.

The first thing you should do is let them know the reason you're reaching out. You need to be as genuine as possible. You can say that you're working on growing your network with like-minded entrepreneurs. Ask them how they got started and be prepared to share a little about you and your business. Refer back to the research you've done.

Here's an example of a message I sent out on Facebook:

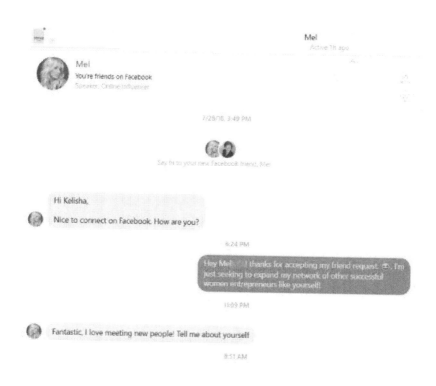

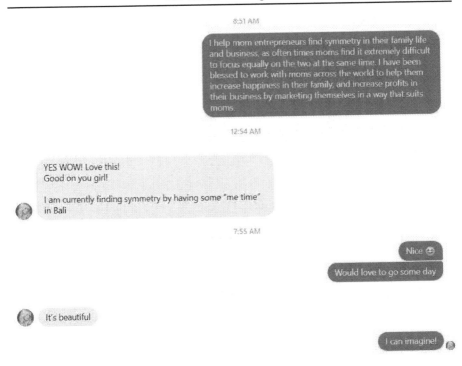

8:51 AM

I help mom entrepreneurs find symmetry in their family life and business, as often times moms find it extremely difficult to focus equally on the two at the same time. I have been blessed to work with moms across the world to help them increase happiness in their family, and increase profits in their business by marketing themselves in a way that suits moms

12:54 AM

YES WOW! Love this!
Good on you girl!

I am currently finding symmetry by having some "me time" in Bali

7:55 AM

Nice 😊

Would love to go some day

It's beautiful

I can imagine!

That's how a genuine conversation is started. Remember, we've never spoken before, however, we have a couple of things in common. We're both moms and entrepreneurs, it'll be much easier to grow from here. Be sure to continue the conversation and follow up every so often.

The same rule can apply for all social media and email platforms. It may be a bit harder to get an email response. Some key influencers don't have a presence on particular social media platforms. If they're not on social media at all, reach out to them through the contact form on their website. Your chances of getting a direct response are much lower, but it's worth the effort.

When I hosted my first online summit, I reached out to well known influencers and I was surprised when I actually received responses. Sometimes, you just have to take a leap and step outside of your comfort zone.

Reaching out can be time consuming. I suggest you create a schedule. Here are a few ideas:

- Separate your list by platform.
- Decide how much time per day you can commit to finding your tribe.
- Use a script for each platform and copy and paste.
- Reach out.
- Set time aside to respond and connect. You could have up to ten conversations going at the same time. Make sure you're prepared.

O: Offer yourself to be of service

Let your newfound contact know how you can be beneficial to their audience. Most social media platforms have an algorithm that works in the favor of the networker. When you send a message and keep in touch, your posts will be one of first they see consistently on their timelines.

This means you must have content prepared to share. Your content must be relevant to your business. No random posts of your family, pets, vacations, meals or rants. You're offering a product or service as a thought leader, influencer and game changer — someone people want to know, like and trust. You must think differently so your new connections will share what you're offering with their friends and network, which is the whole point.

After a few weeks or months, let your new connection know that you're putting out a new product or service and you'd be honored if they would share it with their network. This causes a spider web outreach, and your name will start to trend in different networks. You'll become known as the go-to person in a specific field. This is why you must be clear on who your ideal customer is and connect with a tribe who has a similar audience.

W: Watch your influence and audience grow

This process has worked for me time and time again. I now have connections all over the globe. It's also the reason I'm writing to you in this book. I made a genuine connection with Parul Agrawal, the mastermind behind this project. I'm now connected with over 25 other influencers because of my relationship with her. I can stand as an equal because of our similar fields in entrepreneurship and growth hacking.

Go back to the goal you wrote down in the beginning of this chapter. Let me know how many new connections you've gained after 30 days of implementing this growth hacking method. I promise you, the results will amaze you.

AUTHOR BIOGRAPHY

Kelisha Mills is a wife, mom of four and an Entrepreneur. She resides in the Caribbean Island of Trinidad & Tobago. She has been an entrepreneur since 2007. With over 11 years of experience as a woman entrepreneur, Kelisha knows that she has much to share with other women like herself. She has worked with some of the best international High Performance Coaches and mentors. Kelisha has a strong passion to see women become successful entrepreneurs, which is why she formed Kingdom Women International, a personal development company.

She has hosted online and live workshops geared towards Entrepreneurship and Time Management. She has written numerous exclusive articles and blogs for organizations and prominent websites like BossBabe. She has spoken at live events focused on women's empowerment and self-love. Kelisha specializes in life makeovers for women entrepreneurs, helping them gain the clarity and confidence they need to find symmetry so they can run a successful business and have quality time with their families.

Where to Find Kelisha
www.kelishamills.com

"GROW:
G – Get to know your tribe
R – Reach out
O – Offer yourself to be of service
W – Watch your network increase"

USING OKR STRATEGY FOR SUCCESS IN BUSINESS

By Shailendra Mishra

Young entrepreneurs comprise 70% of the population in India. To provide them with better guidance for their skill-development, an idea struck me. A few of my college friends and I collaborated to work on this idea and Designcut was born.

Designcut provides professional training and workshops in robotics and programming and develops innovative products in conjunction with a few subsidiary companies. Designcut also collaborates with schools and colleges to administer various training programs in technical fields. We also provide training to individual students interested in learning about deep learning, data analysis, robotics, automobile and IC engine type technical topics.

Designcut has two subsidiary firms: Samvaadam and The Engineer's Shop. Samvaadam is a talk show that brings together like-minded, young and budding entrepreneurs to share their engaging stories and inspire others to pursue their dreams and aspirations. The Engineer's Shop is an online app that sells and delivers electronic components for projects to build drone, robotics projects, deep learning integrated robotics, electric vehicles, RPA (Robotic Process Automation) and DIY projects such as student racing cars. It offers the best available price, quick delivery and product reliability.

Our entrepreneurial journey didn't start smoothly. Like every startup, we had to find our identity, our own space and our own work ethics. In the beginning, we were lacking the proper systems to track our progress. For instance, we didn't keep track of the number of people who attended our first few events. There was no strategy in place, no feedback or suggestions could be given to the marketing team to gauge our performance.

This had to change. We then started employing the 'Objective and Key Results Strategy' or OKR. OKR is the tool behind Google's astronomical growth. It is used to track progress as teams move towards achieving objectives that are ambitious and in alignment with the entire organization.

The first thing we had to do was to establish an objective, which was to increase the turnout at our events. In order to do this we established certain key results. To help with this, the marketing department was asked to leave a specific number of impressions across our social media channels to reach a certain amount of people. Once these two key results were achieved, we evaluated the difference it made to our objective of increasing the turn out.

"In our experience, the three essential components, which make every organization growth oriented, are accountability, transparency and the streamlining of goals." #TheGrowthHackingBook #GrowthHackingMovement #GrowthHackingDay"

For the next event, our turnout did go up, however not as much as we wanted it to. For the following events, our objective remained the same, though this time, we settled on more challenging key results. We doubled the amount of social media impressions and increased the amount of people to be reached. Even though our key results weren't achieved in their totality, our objective was accomplished. This time, the relative increase in our turnout was way more than the initial increase in our turnout. Through all of this, an important lesson was learned. We learned the importance of OKR's and how they helped us track our progress, align our business and move towards growth.

In our experience, the three essential components, which make every organization growth oriented, are: accountability, transparency and the streamlining of goals. At Designcut, we achieve these components by incorporating the Objective and Key Results (OKR strategy), formalized by John Doerr, who is one of the most successful venture capitalists of all time. He started his career at Intel and went on to invest in companies such as Google and Amazon.

Every individual in our organization sets their own objectives and subsequent key results within a specific time frame and every quarter, each individual presents their OKR reports to management.

This allows us to align our organization and make sure everyone is heading towards the same big picture goals. Every quarter gives us a chance to review and understand the individual and collective progress where an OKR grade is given. An ideal OKR grade would be somewhere between 60%-70%. A grade higher than this would tell us that our goals aren't ambitious enough. OKRs work in a cyclical manner so low grades are used to refine the next OKRs.

Every employee sets their own Objective and Key Results and puts a plan in place to achieve them. This helps us to keep track of each employee and the organization's progress. Every employee's OKR is made available to everyone in the organization. This allows each employee to integrate their objective with each distinct department and work more coherently as a team. This team spirit not only increases efficiency but also evokes inspiration as they move together in order to achieve a common goal.

Setting OKRs has allowed us to have open communication and transparency with our organization's goals and direction. It sets expectations amongst departments and employees to help increase accountability.

An important factor that should influence objectives is the prevailing conditions in a company's environment. For instance, at Designcut, our objective is centered on youth. This is because India has the largest population of youth in the entire globe. This creates a perfect market for our products, which are directly related to technology. In addition, our company also anticipates the upcoming job market and requirements and keeps that in mind when establishing our objectives.

Our first objective was to expand our technical mentorship program to include more students in India and to grow as a company. In order to achieve our objectives, the key results were decided on. These included reaching more than 10,000 students and increasing revenue from Rs. 20,000 per month to Rs. 2 to 3 lakhs per month. As the key results are realized and our objective met, we could allow ourselves to be more ambitious and set higher objectives and new key results.

On an individual level, every employee is taught about the OKR strategy and its importance to our company as soon as they are recruited. They are then asked to come up with their own objective and respective key results. These are established in a way that directly helps the company's OKRs. The alignment of goals in any organization depends on having a team focused on continuous growth. The only thing holding an organization together is their own perspective and the expectations they've set for the company.

A team's vision could be different from the employer's vision. To keep our employees motivated, aligned and dedicated, they're given monthly incentives. The growth of a startup depends on the growth of the team, which means there should be incentives incorporated into the salary and the physical facilities. To conclude, we feel that our company's growth is directly proportional to team growth.

Companies like Google and Intel also employ the OKR strategy. In order to make their key results measurable, Google uses a scale of 0 to 1.0. Other companies using OKRs include Uber and YouTube. Uber's objective was to increase the number of drivers in their system. In order to achieve this objective, two observable and measurable key results were established: the first being to increase the driver base by 20% and the other being to increase driver average session to 26 hours/weekly in all active regions.

YouTube's objective was to increase viewership minutes because a fixed percentage of time is devoted to ads. As the total viewing time goes up, so do revenues.

Objective: To Increase the Average Watch Time Per User

Key results: assuming we've been tracking the viewing time, it could be:

- Increase total viewership time to XX minutes daily
- Expand native YT application to 2 new OSs
- Reduce video loading times by X%

The first key result sets the metric goal to achieve the objective. Certainty is crucial to achieving the target and if the target is achieved easily then the goals weren't challenging enough.

As demonstrated, OKRs can be useful for startups such as ours, as well as established companies like YouTube, Google and Uber. Many companies are now adopting the OKR methodology. Establishing and following through with OKRs can allow a company to rise to newer heights.

AUTHOR BIOGRAPHY

Shailendra Kumar Mishra has a background in Mechanical Engineering from NIT Uttarakhand. In 2016 he went to Boeing IIT Kanpur for Aeromodelling Training, which inspired him to start his own company. "Designcut" defines its foundation pillars as innovation, information and intelligence with a vision of transforming learning modules of training organizations.

Shailendra is collaborating with ATL laboratories set up by NITI Aayog and is mentoring for labs in Bhimtal and Panchkula. He works with many colleges and institutions and provides them with skill-development programs.

His talk show, "Samvaadam" presents the engaging stories of young entrepreneurs. In order to assist the hindrances of engineers, he launched "The Engineer's Shop" application in 2019. His goal is to provide his services globally.

Where to Find Shailendra
www.designcut.in
www.theengineeersshop.in
www.droneyuga.com

"Objective and Key Results (OKR) is a goal system used by Google and others. It's a simple tool that helps to create alignment and engagement around measurable goals."

GUIDELINE TO BECOME A SUCCESSFUL DIGITAL ENTREPRENEUR

By Badr Berrada

Mark Zuckerberg, Jeff Bezos and Elon Musk inspired a new generation of digital entrepreneurs. They have revolutionized the way we interact, shop and communicate. Facebook, Amazon and PayPal have become essential in our daily life. They believed in themselves, their idea. Likewise, you can also create your own success story by believing in your idea. Every digital entrepreneur has to put their great idea through the rigor of careful validation to understand whether they have a winning online business in front of them.

Some points to ponder:

- Can you explain your awesome idea to your local barber?
- How are you going to reach out to your customers?
- Do you have enough finances to invest in your idea?
- Are you ready to start a new adventure on your own?

Brainstorming and Developing your idea:

Birthing the right idea that could potentially disrupt the digital world requires a good understanding of your strengths and weaknesses. You also need to master sales techniques. It's difficult to hire a team and have employees when you are just starting. Hence, it's important to have a good understanding of what it will take to bring your idea to market and eventually find investors for your project.

It's important to be at ease with your idea. You might not be able to hire people right off the bat. Hence, it's important to understand from top to bottom how you are going to develop and sell your idea before hiring and finding investors. You need to find the gap in your industry and make sure that you are filling it by providing amazing customer service, unique products & services to keep people coming back.

Get your creativity flowing by considering the businesses you rely on in your daily life. Survey people to understand their pain point and then provide solutions accordingly. Some of the most successful digital ideas arose from unmet needs. Watch TED talks, pick up magazines you've never read before, read books on a daily basis to expand on your idea. Your website can very easily be turned into an actual online business: from selling e-books to building online stores and cryptocurrencies, there are numerous ways that you can use your knowledge about a specific niche and convert it into a lucrative business.

It's important to bear in mind that it's never a good idea to ask friends and family to validate your business. They will always respond positively. Only real target customers will provide you the right answers.

The number one piece of advice I would have for someone looking to start an online business today is, "don't quit." This sounds so simple, but I have seen many people giving up within six months of starting a new venture. Success doesn't happen overnight and persistence always pays. It took years for Instagram to grow and achieve the success they've found recently. By sticking with a core concept and brand identity, they eventually achieved the results they wanted.

No matter what business stage you're in, smart growth is key for guaranteeing a solid future for your company. Fostering a strong, healthy and sustainable mindset is essential to survive as an entrepreneur. #GrowthHackingBook #GrowthHackingDay #GrowthHacking

Creating a solid business plan

A solid business plan is one of the most valuable resources for launching any new business venture whether it is physical or online. Just like your first attempt at coding a website, practicing your pitch, or riding a bike, your first business plan is not going to be perfect.

- How will you convince people to invest in your business?
- How long will it take to scale your company?
- How will your venture make a profit?

A business plan has the answer to all these questions to attract potential investors and customers. These days business plans are used as an internal roadmap for the execution of the company since pitch decks have taken over when it comes to fundraising required materials. A good business plan must include an executive summary, company description, products & services, marketing plan, operational plan, management & organization, financial plan and appendices.

Even if you'll never use your business plan to attract investors and raise capital, it can be a vital tool to improve your business. Do your best!! Get outside input from experts and previous entrepreneurs. Get it done, start taking action and stay flexible.

Selling and monetizing online

Finding the right formula to sell online takes time. It's important to combine your sales and marketing skills to craft unique strategies.

If you are a content provider, you can sign up for Google Adsense, Infolinks or Media.net to monetize your traffic. You can also use affiliate marketing by partnering with brands and businesses to promote their content on your website. You could also monetize your video content through sponsorship deals.

Recruiting and motivating employees

Hiring the right people who believe in your vision is a challenge for start-ups. Often it is an after-thought as the focus is almost entirely on getting the product or service to market, launching the brand and raising capital. Share your story and make your team aware of the exponential growth opportunity and they will be equally invested in your company as you are.

Joining a rising start-up with fewer employees means a greater opportunity to do more and to have a bigger impact. True leadership talent doesn't want to be a cog in the wheel of a large organization. Have a defined mission. Let sought-after candidates know your company's potential.

When you can't compete on salary, benefits or name recognition, compete by offering employment that is mission-driven, that rewards results and that is flexible. Offer the chance to build something, to have an impact and to be a key player in something. Someone who is motivated by that offering is someone a protective start-up founder can confidently delegate to.

Fostering a successful company culture

Your culture is your identity. It conveys your shared values, style as a firm, how you work, your design, how you interact with each other and the outside world, how you overcome challenges and celebrate successes, are all part of your company culture. It is always reviewed by investors and something that is very much taken into consideration during due diligence before the investment.

Keep lines of communication open among departments to help your organization work together more fluidly. Being able to leverage different resources internally creates an environment of collaboration and breaks down silos to work toward our overall revenue goal for the year. For better communication, hold a quick weekly stand up to recap the highlights of each business unit. Hire people from diverse backgrounds to create a healthy mix of ideas and experiences.

It's important to invest in productivity tools. For example, if someone is accustomed to using a PC at home but uses a Mac at work, they might feel their workflow is disrupted because they are spending time adjusting to a different computer, rather than focusing on their job. Encourage your employees to suggest new tools they feel would enable greater efficiencies and allow them to make a bigger difference.

The dark side of entrepreneurship: Overcoming odds and obstacles

Most of your friends and family members will discourage you to become a digital entrepreneur, not because they hate you, it's simply because they do not believe in you. It takes guts to launch an online business. You have to bear in mind that you are going to lose loved ones in order to succeed. Being an entrepreneur involves making a lot of sacrifices. If you feel like you are living on the edge of a knife, you are not alone.

You will go through several sleepless nights, experience depression and fear failure. Fostering a strong, healthy and sustainable mindset is essential to survive in the wild. No matter where you are in your entrepreneurial journey, remember that setbacks, loneliness, darkness and hopelessness are part of the game. Giving up should not exist in your dictionary.

My family and soulmate Selma played a huge part in my daily motivation. Nobody is going to believe in you if don't believe in yourself.

Leapfrogging your competitors

Everybody wants an edge. Even if you're among the lucky ones that thrive, there are no guarantees for the future. The best way to beat your competition is to create a killer product or service, sell it in a unique, delight your customers, take their feedback and do it all profitably. Simply being good enough and word of mouth is not enough to survive let alone outsmart your competition.

If you want to be number one, you have to think outside of the box. Consumers' attention span has decreased. They are impatient and will not give you a second chance. Outspending your competitors is expensive, and rarely works. Outsmart them instead by creating a unique company built on purpose and passion. It's more profitable and much more exciting.

Map out your competitors' strengths and weaknesses to take them down.

Use available online tools to penetrate the market, apply SEO techniques and invest a lot in your digital reputation to blindside the competition. Seize on all possible opportunities that will open up for you. If there aren't, create yours.

You do not have to fight every battle that comes your way. By taking arming yourself with business intelligence, you will be able to choose your battles. Never lose heart. The battle is long and arduous. That is a given. But if you will maintain your courage and determination, no obstacle will ever be insurmountable.

Consistency and scaling your business

No matter the stage you're at in your business, smart growth is key for guaranteeing a solid future for your company. After all, while increasing revenue streams can add to your income, it also requires internal expansion within the company itself. Don't be afraid to fine-tune your positioning if something needs to change.

You can always incentivize your current customers to share your brand with special discounts, free service offers or even affiliate programs. As you drive customer growth and fine-tune your company's internal structures, you can scale successfully and plan for lasting success.

AUTHOR BIOGRAPHY

Badr Berrada is an Alum of the London School of Economics with a Masters in Economy, Risk and Society, and holds a Bachelor in Finance from Cass Business School. He's the 24-year-old Founder and CEO of BBN Times. Since launching in Q2 of 2017, his start-up has achieved 14 million page views by 6.6 Million users.

He's a huge advocate of providing a platform and voice to anyone willing to learn more about the latest business trends. Badr has partnered with over 150 experts from all around the world to write genuine, and unbiased content. Each BBN contributor is a global influencer, CEO, Board Member, Government Official, LinkedIn Top Voice or International Best-Seller.

Several BBN Times' articles have been featured in higher education institutions such as Harvard Business School, Massachusetts Institute of Technology (MIT), University of Pennsylvania, New York University and ESSEC Business School.

A self-confessed puzzle seeker and lifelong learner, Badr personifies hard work, honesty, performance, and achievement. Coupled with a positive outlook and an innate curiosity to problem-solve, Badr uses these traits to inspire others.

Where to Find Badr
www.linkedin.com/in/badrberrada
www.bbntimes.com

Outspending your competitors is expensive, and rarely works. The best way to beat your competition is to create a killer product or service.

HOW TO CREATE FINANCIAL GROWTH BY BEING YOUR FEARLESS SELF

By Noam Kostucki

Oscar Wilde said, "Be yourself, everyone else is taken".

The only thing that no one can ever beat you at is 'being you'. Others can be amazing copycats but there is only one original you and no one can compete with that.

I started my corporate career as a skills trainer, teaching marketing strategies, sales techniques and methods that influence buying decisions. I moved to helping entrepreneurs and businesses, by consulting and designing websites and creating customer acquisition campaigns for my clients.

Despite getting great results, it wasn't the best use of my time and my clients' money. We were expending a lot of effort, when I could see another, more efficient path.

I noticed that successful people figure out strategic and tactical solutions to their problems, and what my clients really needed to achieve their goals was someone to help them go deeper and focus on the internal blocks that are stopping them from taking the right actions. With one-on-one coaching I have helped many clients, company Founders, Investors, Creators and Artists, to overcome these blocks and move forward to create massive success.

Client Example 1

One of my clients, Patryk needed to raise $250,000 to make a documentary. When we talked, in the three months prior, he was not able to raise any money at all. During our conversation, I identified the mental block that was stopping him from taking action to achieve this goal.

I recommended he change his approach from asking for $1,000 to $5,000 from potential investors, to asking for $250,000. It sounded counter intuitive and his first reaction was, "If people don't want to give me $1,000, it makes no sense to ask them for $250,000."

I encouraged him to trust the process and go ahead and ask for $250,000 and he agreed. A few weeks later I received an email thanking me because with the strategy I recommended, he had raised his first $130,000, from only two people.

After four months I heard from him again as he had not been able to raise any money since we last spoke. We began one-on-one coaching and after only eight weeks, Patryk had raised a total of $750,000.

We made three critical upgrades:

1. We aligned his documentary 100% with his personality and the essence of who he is.
2. We redesigned his offers to be an outrageous extension of his personality.
3. We worked on his mindset, approach to situations and communication skills.

Client Example 2

When I worked with Esther on her TED Talk, which became one of the '30 most viewed' TED Talks of all time, we focused her talk on the idea, 'what you are most scared to say and how to say it in the most honest and loving way'.

This strategy involved having Esther focus on the core of who she is and being herself in an outrageous and loving way.

The best strategies are not always clear right away, they are not always what you would expect should be done, and they are sometimes, not even logical.

Every time I start a new venture, people tell me, "You're crazy," "This makes no business sense" or "How the fuck do you think this is ever going to work?"

Every time, I do the same thing and bypass logic by focusing my attention on creating a deep internal alignment. When you create something that's truly aligned with who you are at the core, you end up with a product or service that sells itself.

By doing what's logical and expected, you can only get results that are logical and expected. If you want extraordinary results, you must do something extraordinary.

Be YOU In Business 3-Step Formula

1. Who Are You?

How are you unique and different?

What is it about you that makes you, "YOU"?

When you find the core of who you are, growth happens naturally. This first part of the process becomes apparent with introspection and self-awareness, through meditation, deep conversations, personal reflection, active exploration and research.

Recently, I spoke with one of my closest friends about her job at a bank. Even though she is great at her job, if she were to leave, her employer would find someone else, to do what she does. They will find someone who gives equivalent results, because *what she does* at her job is replaceable.

Now she is looking for what it is that only she can do, that which makes her unique and different from everyone else.

When you know yourself deeply, everything else flows in a natural way. The sun doesn't try hard to shine light and warmth. It doesn't put forth effort to make the planets revolve around it. If the sun weren't a warm shining light, with planets revolving around it, it wouldn't be the sun it would be something else.

Trees don't struggle to be trees. They convert carbon dioxide to oxygen because that's what trees are about. In the same way, there is something about you that is unique to you. There is something about how you think and who you are that is effortless and natural to you.

"The only thing that no one can ever beat you at is 'being you'." #TheGrowthHackingBook #GrowthHackingMovement #GrowthHackingDay

2. How Do You Add Value?

Once you discover who you are, the next step is to translate your being into the value you give to others. The idea is to exchange something of high value to your clients, for something that is of low value to you. Through trial and error, quick iteration, feedback from customers and market research you will find the perfect high value offer for your clients, that costs you little to create, and is an extension of the real you.

What product or service can you create that's a representation of you, one that is intrinsically you?

What can you offer to your clients that gives much more value to them, than it costs to create?

3. How Do You Sustain Growth?

Growth hacking implies an ability to sustain growth. The problem businesses have as they grow, is maintaining the quality of their products and services. What built their initial success becomes their downfall. Focusing on growth hacking without a growth strategy is more harmful than helpful.

The idea of creating something that has infinite growth is a misconception that can kill the soul of a business, product or service.

The important question is: How much growth can you sustain while keeping heart, soul and uniqueness in your business?

Apple Computers has continued to create new products and services that carry the essence of its Founder, Steve Jobs. What was created often didn't make sense, like computers without floppy disks, and laptops without CD and DVD players and yet they have become standards in the industry. Other computer companies copied Apple because they created something outrageous from a place of love that was an extension of its Founder. In that sense Apple continues to reinvent itself by creating products and services that sell themselves.

I've applied these strategies when working with clients as well as in growing my own business. As a result, I've been invited to speak at Harvard University about entrepreneurship; my first book, *You Are Your Brand*, became required reading at the Fashion Institute of Technology; and my third book, *Seek To Keep: How to Find the Best Mentors and Keep Them*, was featured in the Stanford Technology Venture Program.

AUTHOR BIOGRAPHY

Noam is an explorer, a creator and a guide. He loves to try new experiences that push him beyond his limits and then create similar adventures where he can guide others. In everything he is and does, Noam is naturally drawn to integrating opposites. This is why his company is called: HiR... The integration of 'Him' and 'Her'.

His most recent successful creation is HiR Fine Dining, a restaurant in Noam's home of Costa Rica. In two years HiR Fine Dining became #1 on OpenTable & TripAdvisor. With no formal culinary training and never having worked in a restaurant before, within six months of opening, one of Noam's own plate creations was selected by OpenTable as, "One of 25 Dishes to Travel Around the World For".

Over the years, Noam has worn many different hats, from Art Photographer to Judo Coach and Web Designer. His main professional background for the past 15 years is in Business Coaching. Noam has helped over 25,000 people from all around the world, to grow successful businesses, charities, government organizations and social enterprises.

At the age of 23 Noam's TED Talk, "Selfishness is the Best Reason to Cooperate", Noam received the 'UK Business Speaker of the Year Runner Up' award. Noam's first book, *You Are Your Brand*, became required reading at the Fashion Institute of Technology in NYC and his third book, *Seek To Keep: How to Find the Best Mentors and Keep Them*, was featured in the Stanford Technology Venture Program, along with many other features and accolades.

Today, Noam lives Costa Rica where he coaches entrepreneurs and creators to make money while living magical lives. He cooks at his home for guests from all over the world.

His most recent new project is HiR Transcenders, an entrepreneurship program and network of investors for transgender and non-binary people.

Where to Find Noam
www.hiradventure.com
www.facebook.com/noamkostucki
Instagram: @noamkos

"Incorporate your uniqueness into the value you offer your customers. It's about creating a product or service that's an extension of you."

Build A Celebrity Brand & Raise An Army Of Light

By Evita Ramparte

————◆————

I get you. Sometimes you feel so awkward in this world that it makes you feel as if you are an Extra-Terrestrial sent here to Earth by some more advanced civilization. I have news for you: You Probably Are!!

You carry a dream within you: a possibility, a solution for the multitude of beings on this Planet and you seek to deliver the Message.

It's tough. Nobody really cares you are a Cosmic VIP and those who sent you here forgot to send a Ferrari. Worst of all, no matter how much you try to shrink and squeeze in, you can't seem to fit in this world. The more you try, the more it feels awkward like pushing a circle into a square.

I've been there. It was a pain. I kept missing the target.

Until, I pulled out my own 'Deck of Cards' and began to play my own Game with a radically different set of Rules:

Rule #1. I make my own Rules.

Rule #2. Questions? Look at Rule No 1.

First and foremost, I decided I am not here to 'fit in'; I am here to change things.

Second of all, I am getting paid for causing change.

I gave up all efforts at fitting into this insane reality and started to place expert value on my own unique contribution to cause change. I quickly realized that I provide a life-changing value far beyond what can be bought in any store.

I became a relentless Vortex of Transformation. Transformation became my second name. I chose to believe I change people's lives just by showing up in their lives, by frequency. Today I have no doubt, molecules rearrange when I walk into a room. Why? Because I say so. My Word creates a new reality and calls forth new possibilities.

As much as I'd love to help everyone, not everyone is ready and my life would be a disaster if I made myself available to everyone. I had to pick and choose who I wanted to help, why and how. It was clear to me that I wanted to raise New Leaders and let the change trickle down. I realized in order to communicate to Leaders, I needed to exclude everyone else who did not have a leadership mindset. I observed I am most effective when I operate on the frequency of Joy. It gives my clients and myself a great degree of power and velocity. I needed to become selective and exclusive, when it comes to who I am willing to work with and interact with. Time is of the essence.

I created an Application Funnel, which deliberately discouraged people from applying if they did not resonate on the same wavelength. This proved very effective. Leaders - Celebrities, Athletes and CEOs - want to feel special. They want to know I don't just work with everybody and anybody. They want to know, I'd rather work with very few people, then we have massive success working together. As a result, they had to apply to schedule a meeting with me and they had to prove themselves worthy of my time. I flipped it. Instead of me begging to be hired, I started to be a sought-after consultant.

90% of creating a Celebrity Brand is your own Mindset, your Frequency and your Highest Purpose. Invitations and opportunities when examined by my Heart are very clear — either aligned or not. I chose to do big things or nothing; I give time and energy to things that have meaning to me, or — I don't work. I chill out at the beach with my son, which is a lot of fun. I refuse to function on obligation, duty and guilt. No matter what the state of my bank account is, I refuse to operate from a scarcity mindset and fear.

"90% of creating a Celebrity Brand is your own Mindset, your Frequency and your Highest Purpose." #TheGrowthHackingBook #GrowthHackingMovement #GrowthHackingDay #GrowthHacking

Becoming a Celebrity Brand is all about becoming a Leader. Leaders sense each other. They sense the vibration of possibility and lightness of being that comes from high frequency of faith that's bending waves of reality and manifesting miracles. Leadership is the toughest path of service there is. The world crucifies its Leaders. Leaders are being constantly criticized, laughed at, having tomatoes thrown in their face. Leaders are the subjects of backbiting and jealousy and they have little to no private life. One needs to be 'nuts' to seek that. I learned quickly: to lead is to serve and to serve is to lead.

Celebrity status is not only about the limelight and high life and high-ticket sales. It carries a certain sophisticated presence, a sense of class, an energy, an allure, a mystery. If you follow a Celebrity, it is because they shine like a 'Star' on your life-path. They inspire you to be like them, eat like they do, travel like they do, raise kids like they do, reach for the lifestyle you desire. They show you what's possible for you, if you only choose it. It is your birthright, if you only design your life that way. With elegance and grace, they chart a new horizon of dreams and possibilities for you. They inspire you, you admire them and you give them your attention and your energy. Remember, they need you to keep shining just like you need them to light your path.

A lot could be spoken here about the choice of fonts, colors and images in creating a Celebrity Brand and Sales Funnels. It's clear to you that fonts carry energy. Look at the logos of Porsche and Mazda and you get a slightly different feel. Look at the fonts in Cosmopolitan and in Oprah Magazine, they have a completely different look and feel.

Brand design comes easy and any designer can create this for you, if you only know how unique you are, and how unique your contribution is here on Earth. Your unique energetic signature needs to be translated into the design of your brand. It also needs to reflect the world of those you talk to. Look at the fonts they look at, the cars they own, the art and design that make their world. Meet them where they are and take them with you higher!

A Celebrity is like a King or a Queen. If you maintain a steady, constant energy and emotional balance you will become a Vortex of Transformation and Possibility here on Earth. There will be an increasing motion of energy around you, a hive of fans and followers. They are eager to help you and serve along with you! People are good. They are waiting. They only need leaders to lead them. You need to raise an Army of Light.

The two-step strategy is simple:

1. Identify the Leaders.
2. Lead the Leaders.

Serve the servants. Offer them a platform. Create an exclusive community for them to get the spotlight they deserve. Interview them, connect them, introduce them to each other, help them to lead better, train them and coach them to increase their sense of value for their unique skillset. Let them co-create; let them learn from each other. You hold space for this to happen, you chart the strategy, let them choose their own tactics and watch what happens when the movement you started takes on its own life. This is going to grow. This will be your Legacy on Earth. You will raise Leaders just like You! An Army of Light.

AUTHOR BIOGRAPHY

Evita Ramparte is a European Journalist, Bestselling Author, and Wellness Industry Trendsetter. She helps men and women to achieve peak health and energy, and revive their love life. She is a Health Expert, Karezza Mystic and a trusted Spiritual Sensei to Celebrities, Athletes and CEOs.

She holds two MA Degrees in Comparative Studies of Religion and a Post-graduate Degree in Journalism and Mass Communication. She is a former TV News Reporter and a Contributor to Newsweek and Cosmopolitan.

In 2000, Evita was diagnosed with ovarian cancer and healed herself in a few months, losing over 50 lbs thanks to fasting, forgiveness and high carb raw vegan lifestyle. This experience embarked her on a spiritual journey as a woman. She has studied various healing modalities, transformational coaching systems, nutrition, as well as Neuroscience and Neuro-Endocrynology.

Evita offers private coaching and VIP retreats for individuals seeking to achieve peak health and energy, top brain performance, as well as clarity, connection and commitment in their relationships.

Her teachings result in benefits that reach far beyond physical health and natural beauty, into spiritual awakening, abundance and enlightenment. They promote integrity, high moral values and leadership.

Where to Find Evita
www.evitaramparte.com

How to raise an Army of Light: Identify the Leaders. Lead the Leaders."

TOOLSET

Learn the tools and methods you can use to scale your business and create an impact.

THE ULTIMATE GUIDE ON GENERATING LEADS VIA COLD EMAIL

By Will Cannon

While some business owners and sales reps believe it's near impossible to generate leads via cold email, this simply isn't true. There are multiple case studies which prove you can cold email prospects and get great response rates[1].

If you haven't done so already, you'll definitely want to add cold emailing to your bag of tricks. In this chapter, we walk you through several tips and best practices on cold emailing and teach you how to get the most out of the cold emails that you send.

Identifying the Right Email Recipients

Only email prospects who match your ideal customer persona

When sending out cold emails, never make the mistake of going for quantity over quality. Sure, you can send out 100 emails everyday, but if you're emailing folks who aren't a good fit and would *never* buy your product or service, then you're essentially wasting your time.

Instead, make sure you only email prospects who match your ideal customer persona. If most of your users are IT executives in the USA

---

1   www.singlegrain.com/email-marketing/6-cold-email-case-studies-with-great-reply-rates/

working for companies with 1,000+ employees, for instance, then make sure that's who you're emailing. This gives you a leg up from the get-go, and increases the chances that your prospects will reply.

Find contacts to email using UpLead

How do you find contacts to email? We recommend using UpLead, a tool that helps marketers and business owners build targeted prospect lists. With UpLead, you can search through a database of 46+ million business contacts and hone in on your target audience using 50+ different criteria (industry, job title, sales revenue, number of employees, location, technologies used, and more.)

If you're keen on trying out UpLead, you can get a 7-day free trial at UpLead.com. For those of you who would like to supplement your lead generation efforts with manual research, you can also hire virtual assistants or research assistants on Upwork to put together a list of prospects.

Segment as much as possible to make your messaging relevant

If you can make your cold email (and your offer!) relevant to your prospect, that's half the battle won. To do this, make sure to segment your email list, instead of sending the same generic email to everyone on your list.

Say you've segmented your email list by company size, for example. When you're reaching out to small businesses, you might want to emphasize the fact that your product or service is cost-effective, and brings about a high ROI. In your email to larger conglomerates, you might highlight that you've worked with plenty of Fortune 500 companies and reputable firms and that you provide end-to-end training and support for teams.

Crafting Your Email

Optimize your subject line

Think of your subject line as the gatekeeper to your cold email. If your subject line isn't interesting or compelling enough, your prospect won't read your email, simple as that. Bearing this in mind, it's important to continuously A/B test and optimize your subject lines.

Personally, at UpLead, we find that short email subject lines tend to work best. Two email subject lines that have worked well for UpLead are:

- Quick question
- Hi {FirstName}
- Let's work together, {FirstName}
- YourCompanyName <> Prospect'sCompanyName

That aside, highlighting a key benefit that you can bring to your prospect may also make your subject line more compelling. For instance, this could be along the lines of:

- Still can't hit your sales targets?
- Still struggling to generate leads?
- 250% more leads for {CompanyName} in 6 months.

Keep your email short and sweet

Put yourself in your prospect's shoes. If you open an email and you're greeted by a wall of text, what would you do? Chances are, you'll give up there and then and move on to reading the rest of your emails.

When you're crafting an email (especially a cold email!), be sure to keep your email short and sweet. This applies to both the overall length of your email and the length of individual paragraphs. As a general rule of thumb, keep each paragraph to one to two sentences.

Remember: the point of your initial cold email is simply to make contact, and get your prospect interested in what your company does. You're not trying to sell to them on the spot, so there's no need to send them a long, rambling essay!

Personalize your email

When it comes to personalization, don't just reference your prospect's name in your email and call it a day. You should also go one step further in personalizing your emails based on your prospects' location, company, background, the schools they went to, etc.

For instance, if your prospect is from Michigan and you know the area has been experiencing erratic weather, ask them about that. If your prospect happens to have attended the same school that you did, bring that up - it'll help you build rapport and hopefully get a foot in the door.

Include all the relevant information

Every cold email should consist of the following information:

- Who you are and how you found your prospect
- Why you're reaching out and what you're offering
- A clear Call To Action (book a demo, sign up for a trial, set up a meeting, etc.)

The last element - the Call To Action, is particularly important. The onus is on you to make the process as clear and straightforward for your prospect as possible and you don't want your prospect to get all the way to the end of your email, then think: *Now what?*

Talk about how you can help your prospect

When cold emailing, many marketers and business owners fall into the trap of talking about themselves too much. Keep in mind that doing this makes your prospects lose interest and lowers your chance of getting a response.

What should you do instead? Simple. Tell your prospect what you can do for them and communicate the value that you bring to the table. Assuming that you've assessed their business needs accurately, this is a great way of reeling them in and getting them interested.

Formatting Your Email

Keep the format simple

A cold email is NOT a newsletter so there's no need to utilize a fancy template when sending your cold emails. Remember: the more HTML you have in your emails, the higher the chances of your email going to the "Promotions" tab instead of "Primary". If you're unlucky, your email might even land in your prospect's Spam folder.

The bottom line? While you can include images and videos (which we'll discuss shortly), the bulk of your email should be in plain text. It should not contain a ton of HTML; nor should it be formatted like a newsletter.

Stand out with images and videos

We don't recommend using fancy, over-the-top templates, but it's perfectly fine to add a few images or videos to your cold emails. This helps add visual interest and breaks up monotony.

For instance, some marketers send their prospects emails titled "Message for {FirstName}", and include video introductions of themselves in these emails. Note that these videos don't have to be corporate videos, if you use a video that's less 'polished', and looks like it was taken from your own webcam, this might help with your response rates.

Sending Your Email

SPAM test your email before sending

At the basic level, you'll want to avoid using spam-like words in your emails and keep the text to HTML ratio high; this will reduce your chances of getting flagged as spam. On top of that, you can also use tools such as GlockApps.com and Mail-tester.com to check your reputation and authentication and find out whether your emails are getting delivered to the major Internet Service Providers (ISPs).

Verify your emails

BriteVerify is an award-winning email validation service that helps you ensure that you're sending your cold emails to accurate, verified email addresses. If you use a reputable tool such as UpLead to find prospects to email, you shouldn't have any problem with email accuracy.

If you bulk-buy lists of email addresses for cheap, on the other hand, you might find that most of the emails on your list are outdated, and will result in hard bounces. To prevent this from affecting your email deliverability, run your emails through BriteVerify first, so you can filter out the invalid ones.

Fun fact: UpLead uses real-time email verification, which allows users to verify the contact information of prospects right before they unlock and download said information. All the contacts on UpLead's database also come with a 97% accuracy guarantee.

"If you don't receive a reply to your first cold email, don't give up. Send at least two to four follow-ups over a month or so." #TheGrowthHackingBook #GrowthHackingMovement #GrowthHackingDay

Automate your sending

To be frank, cold emailing takes a lot of effort. With each prospect that you want to reach out to, you've got to personalize your email, send it out to them, then follow up if they don't respond. Luckily, there are several tools that you can use to automate the process, such as lemlist, Woodpecker, Mailshake and Reply.io. With these tools, you can personalize multiple emails, all at once and you don't have to manually edit and send each email.

A/B Testing Your Emails

A/B testing your cold emails will help you improve open rates and response rates and bring you more success.

Here are a few ways in which you can A/B test your cold emails:

1. Email subject title
2. Call To Action (CTA): Type of CTA
3. CTA: The number of times you repeat the CTA
4. Images vs no images
5. Videos vs no videos
6. Send time
7. Send day
8. Benefits: highlight different benefits
9. Framing: framing in a positive or negative light
10. Follow ups: number of follow ups
11. Follow ups: timing/day of follow ups
12. Follow ups: reiterating existing content vs adding new content

Additional Tips to Keep in Mind

Follow up persistently

When you're sending cold emails, it's unlikely that your prospects will reply to you immediately. If you don't receive a reply, don't give up, send at least two to four follow-ups over a month or so. Don't worry, you won't have to do this manually. Once you've sent your initial email, you can easily configure the email automation tools we mentioned earlier to trigger follow up messages on day four, day seven, day 12, etc.

Improve email deliverability

You can do a number of things to ensure that your email deliverability is high. First, make sure your send volume is more or less consistent. You can use lemlist (or any of the other tools mentioned earlier) to spread out your email sending over a period of time.

On top of that, set up your Sender Policy Framework (SPF), DomainKeys Identified Mail (DKIM) and your own tracking domain correctly. Last but not least, make sure that your domain has been warmed up properly before you start sending emails in bulk, and check that you haven't been blacklisted on mxtoolbox.

Use personalized landing pages

Many marketers and business owners assume that your cold emails are all about the emails but that's where they're wrong. Emails aside, you'll also have to ensure that your landing pages are well crafted and consistent with your emails. Think of it this way: once your prospect clicks through from your email to your landing page, it's up to the landing page to reduce any friction on the prospect's part and encourage them to convert.

How do you do this? First, make sure you use the exact same headers or terminology on your cold email and landing pages, so there's a message-match. This makes it easy for your prospect to process the information on your page and reduces the chances they'll be confused. On top of that, personalize the page based on the prospect's needs and situation and make sure you have a strong CTA on the page.

A final word on generating leads via cold email

If you're intimidated at the thought of reaching out to prospects via cold email, don't be. At the end of the day, remember that you're bringing value to your prospect with your company's product or service, and helping them achieve their goals. What are you waiting for? Start crafting and sending out those cold emails today!

AUTHOR BIOGRAPHY

Will Cannon is the founder and CEO of the B2B sales intelligence platform UpLead. UpLead is a tool that allows businesses to identify and reach out to their ideal customers with ease.

Where to Find Will
www.linkedin.com/in/will-cannon
twitter.com/iamwillcannon
Or directly by email: william@uplead.com

"To prevent invalid emails from affecting your email deliverability, run your emails through BriteVerify first, and filter out the invalid ones."

How To Create An Army Of 1000 Micro-Influencers In 30 Days Who Will Sell For You

By Deep Kakkad

———◆———

First things first, the best growth-hack I can give you is: Hack your brain to think about growth in an out-of-the-box way. If you crack that, you'll crack growth, marketing, productivity, hiring and any other area in business that you can think of. Understanding this will help you implement the strategies from this chapter, in your business to get surprising results. I promise.

Before we move into the implementation phase, I'll tell you how using this method led me to acquire 1,000 micro-influencers, 1,000 email addresses, over 6,000 website visitors, a ton of sales and better brand exposure. It only cost me a little bit of effort, a one-month marketing campaign and $47. I'll teach you how to do this without spending a penny.

This chapter shares the secret sauce to creating an army of micro-influencers, referred to as ambassadors, that you can use for all types of businesses. I will use a fictional business called "Growth Hack Academy" to demonstrate the process that you can easily use for your own business.

Let's say you're the owner and the CMO (Chief Marketing Officer) of Growth Hack Academy, a business that sells online courses. Your job as the owner is to create courses that help established businesses and new startups learn growth hacking. Your job as a marketer is to sell your courses. As a marketer, your marketing channels might include social media, an email list, Facebook advertisements and content marketing. Using all of these platforms means you'll be putting forth a lot of effort and cash.

Do you know what's the best and most effective marketing channel? A referral. One way to get referrals is to create an army of ambassadors by running a win-win contest.

Contest participants are two types of people:

1. People who are really interested in your courses.
2. People who want to win contests for the rewards.

Now what are these rewards, you ask? As the owner of Growth Hack Academy, you'll have to leverage a small portion of your assets to give away to the contestants for their efforts and to convert them into ambassadors, and make it a win for both of you.

Let's talk about the type of rewards you can offer your contestants and the efforts ambassadors will put forward to help your company. As a suggestion, it's a good idea to understand the lifetime value of a customer is to your business and base your rewards on that.

Examples of rewards:

- 25% or 50% off discount for their choice of a Growth Hack Academy's course.
- A certificate of ambassadorship or certificate of participation.
- A most influential ambassador award.
- A free coaching session with Growth Hack Academy.
- A free Growth Hack Academy course.

- A mention or promotion in Growth Hack Academy's social media pages and newsletter.
- Winner's choice of any Growth Hack Academy merchandise.
- A chance to become an affiliate and earn commissions for Growth Hack Academy.
- Free access to all courses and materials of Growth Hack Academy for a limited amount of time.

If you haven't noticed already, most of these rewards don't cost much but mean a lot to your contestants. This is a win for them.

Examples of How This Contest Will Benefit Growth Hack Academy:

- Contestants will submit their email address and subscribe to the newsletter.
- Ask contestants to follow Growth Hack Academy on social media to increase your following.
- Ask contestants to share on social media and to invite other contestants to increase your following.
- Ask contestants to share your courses on social media to increase your sales.

But how do you keep track of all this activity? Be at ease, because there are tools that will do the tracking and even rewarding for you. One such tool is, Vyper. Remember when I told you it cost me only $47 for one month?

Vyper is a hosting site that lets you create a luring landing page where people sign-up to become brand ambassadors. It redirects people to a leaderboard and a list of tasks to complete. These tasks include any in the above list. As the contestants complete these tasks, they accumulate points, which are predetermined by you, and convert to rewards at the end of the contest.

A free alternative to Vyper is KingSumo but it has less features. As the owner of Growth Hack Academy, I recommend you buy Vyper if you anticipate 1000 contestants sharing your courses on their social media. Even if this contest converts one customer, it's worth the $47.

If you just want to test the process or run a contest for your email subscribers, which won't gain you monetary benefits, KingSumo is a good option.

How to get traction to your ambassador contest?

Here's a cool trick that'll help you with your advertising. This is my go-to when I advertise. This is what we call 'Hack your competitors traffic".

Find competitors by searching Google for "Growth hack courses" and similar keywords. See who is advertising on Google and look for other listings on Google search results.

Go to similarweb.com to check where their traffic is coming from.

Check your analytics to find out where traffic for Growth Hack Academy is coming from.

From the list of websites that send traffic to Growth Hack Academy, find content sites that are sending traffic to competitors.

Contact those traffic sources and tell them about your contest. Ask for a special advertising discount to offer your contest to their audience on their website.

The best part about an ambassador and referral contest is that it only takes ignition. Once ignited, it grows itself. You pick a few ambassadors, they invite their friends and it keeps going and growing exponentially. If your goal is to reach between 10,000 - 50,000 ambassadors, it's best to advertise.

Handpick your first ambassadors and influencers. It helps to talk to a few influencers before you run your contest to get them prepared to participate.

If you want to attract mid level influencers, offer them a reward upfront. In the case of Growth Hack Academy, free access to all your courses would be a great motivator.

> *"Offer incentives to create win-win scenarios for you and your Brand Ambassadors." #TheGrowthHackingBook #GrowthHackingMovement #GrowthHackingDay*

Understand that you can't expect this level of influencer to do the selling for you or continuously share your courses to their entire network. Your goal is to get them to share your contest once when it's launched and your job is to reward them for it. When contacting them initially, let them know that you're aiming to give away a lot of your content to enthusiastic people, and give them a way to share your contest in a way that makes them look good. I suggest you to do this a couple of weeks prior to the launch.

To keep your influencers and ambassadors engaged, keep them updated. Create content for them. Give them ideas on how to market better to get more points that they can convert to awesome rewards.

Use an email tool like lemlist.com to create personalized emails. Promote weekly bests in email blasts to give them a competitive push.

You can even create a Facebook community specifically for ambassadors and influencers.

Things to consider while running an ambassador contest

Test before launch. The tools can get complicated and as a result, it could create confusion for participants. Before you launch, go through the process yourself as a contest participant and complete a few tasks to make sure the reward system is working the way you want it to.

To be fair, there are no limits to this type of promotion. It works if you're trying to generate B2B leads, get subscribers for your email newsletter or sell a product or service. All you need is a list of rewards and a list of tasks that your ambassadors can accomplish to get the rewards, to help you create an army of influencers and brand ambassadors that will help you reach and sell to more people.

AUTHOR BIOGRAPHY

As a 23-year old entrepreneur, Deep has been named as top 30 game-changers of India. Deep started his entrepreneurial journey at 18 by building a platform that decreased the number of deaths occurring due to unavailability of blood in emergency situations. At 20, after failing another funded startup, deep started working as a marketing consultant (worked with 30+ companies), Deep became a LinkedIn influencer with 3m+ reach till date. He has been mentioned in various books and publications on entrepreneurship. Recently, deep was awarded global entrepreneur in climate changes at an international competition. Now, Deep heads marketing at FinTech School.

Where to Find Deep
www.linkedin.com/in/deepkakkad

"Use the power of ambassadors and influencers to reach a larger audience and sell more products and services."

Automate Workflows To Make Growth Hacking Easy

By Rachit Khator

Planning, managing and automating right are the three most critical steps to your growth hacking journey.

Today, we are all consuming services across multiple channels without realizing what got us here. Understanding this is utmost importance before we wear our creative hats and market on the internet.

Though the World Wide Web was born in the 1980s, the real consumption of digital services happened in 2000, with the introduction of 'Web APIs' by. It didn't take off, until things got Social in 2004 when Flickr first introduced its API that allowed users to embed Flickr photos in blogs and social networks. That was the first growth hack, in my opinion, as it allowed Flickr to open up new business development opportunities via the use of 'Web APIs.' Then Facebook, Twitter and others followed, allowing developers to access their interface to scrape user information, build applications and use it in ways we never imagined before.

The use of 'Web APIs' became real when Amazon launched Amazon Web Services, and Amazon S3, which provided a simple interface to store and retrieve any information from the web — from anywhere. Then followed AWS EC2, first just a RESTful API, which allowed deployment and distribution of services globally. You could now run a business globally using just APIs. It was only after 3 years in 2009, that

Amazon launched a web interface of AWS EC2.

As with many things, the digital strategy came full circle with the introduction to Mobile. It was a game-changer when Apple opened up their App Store with APIs being the driving force. Today, millions of developers build applications on that ecosystem.

Fast forward to the present day — now, the web is full of information and services about people, companies, products, providers, etc., but the usage of those services is still with people who know how to code. They are often out of reach of the non-technical end users. Out of 7.7B people in the world, there are just 22M people who can code — a mere 0.28%.

Stackby is precisely solving this problem, by bringing a familiar spreadsheet-style interface, functionality of databases and best business APIs (MailChimp, Clearbit, YouTube, Twilio, etc.), into a single new cloud-based platform. Now anyone can customize and automate according to their workflows, no coding or training needed.

Irrespective of who you are, the Founder of a tech company, running a marketing agency or a Marketing Manager in a large enterprise, shouldn't computation be accessible to all? Only with that accessibility can growth hacking become a true reality.

Growth hacking is not an art. It's a process and science of getting to repeatable, predictable and scalable outcomes. Behind that science, it's important to plan, manage and automate the experiments in the right way.

But do you need a technical bent of mind to build and measure those growth experiments? What if you are not a programmer who knows the abracadabra of coding? What does it take to run those growth experiments? It could be using different platforms, software, tools to not just plan but also track your growth. What if you could do all these on a single platform? You plan/brainstorm, you jot down ideas, work on, collaborate with your team, check back the status of the plan once it is put in action and track the metrics at a single place. That is exactly how Stackby could help you with your growth hacking.

"Growth hacking is not an art. It's a process and science of getting to repeatable, predictable and scalable outcomes. Behind that science, it's important to plan, manage and automate the experiments in the right way." #TheGrowthHackingBook #GrowthHackingMovement #GrowthHackingDay

Here's a step-wise plan on how you can do it on Stackby:

1. Plan Your Campaigns

It all starts with brainstorming ideas and a list of channels you want to move forward with or let go — in short, keeping track of it. As you work out and process your ideas, you can start jotting them down on a table (grid-style view) on Stackby.com. This allows you to define a process and measure the progress of your growth experiments as you run through each idea.

It's all within rows and columns, but there are over 25 different column types that you can choose from — Text, Dropdowns, Attachments, Link to other Tables, Lookup, Push Buttons and APIs, with multiple new layouts to visualize your campaigns like Kanban or Calendar.

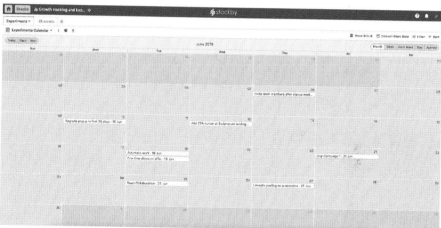

2. Manage Your Marketing Funnel Process

Segment the experiments based on:

- Marketing funnel impact — Acquisition, Activation, Retention, Referrals or Revenues
- Categories — Call to Action, Product Pricing, New Graphics, etc.
- Place — Individual Web Page, Email Campaigns, etc.

3. Collaborate to Keep Things Moving

Assign and monitor your teams' progress on each of the experiments, and track the status in a single cohesive view. Move between the funnels or statuses, chat on each of the experiments and get things done. The idea should be to fail fast, fail cheap and get back on your feet faster.

4. Automate Data to Get Things Done and Track Metrics

Here are few use-cases that you can automate using Stackby to plan, manage and track your experiments effectively:

1. Managing Your Lead Generation Based on the Company, Type and Persona

If you are a B2B company, you can start by creating a lead list based on your ideal customer personas. Say, if you have a list of company domain names, then you can connect your column to a Hunter.io or a Clearbit API service. Choose an Email Finder service that automatically fetches information right inside your stack in Stackby, then all you have to do is refresh the information to bring the latest data. Removes the need for manual data entry.

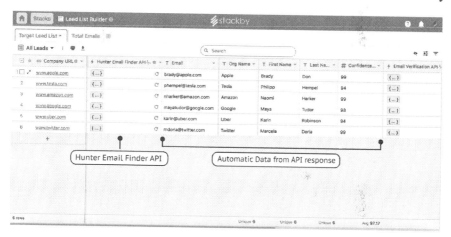

Not just that, you can also choose an Email Verifier service to get a deliverability score and whether that email is deliverable or risky to send.

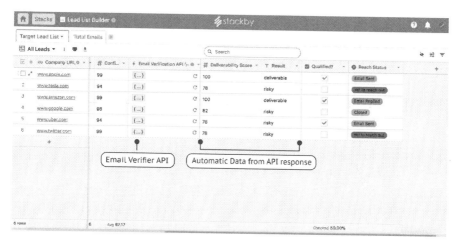

This is how you can automate your lead generation process with a few clicks within Stackby.

2. Enriching the Person and Company Data to Make the Campaigns Relevant

To make sure you send the right content and message to your audience, you need to know your audience well. While it may be time-consuming to do manually, you can get rich information about a company or a person using the FullContact API.

Based on the domain name you can find company information or person name and information about their likes and dislikes, etc. This makes it easy for your Content Team to be as personalized as possible, which makes for better conversions.

You can connect a column type to a FullContact API and reference it to the company or person column to fetch that information directly into your table, now you can take meaningful action.

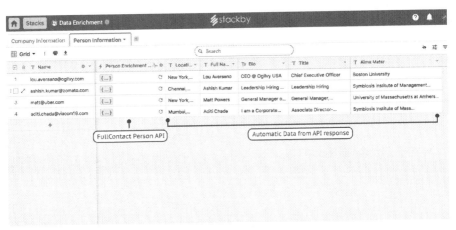

3. Managing Your Email Campaigns with MailChimp Integration

As per the latest research from HubSpot, 93% of B2B marketers use email to distribute content; active email accounts are expected to hit 5.9 billion by 2019. This means that email is still one of the most relevant and highly used marketing channels. Whether it is a drip campaign, personalized reach-outs, e-newsletters or mailers, they are all relevant campaign strategies to drive conversations.

It is important that you plan and manage and also that you track your email campaign metrics and optimize your efforts as you run growth experiments.

You can use Stackby to connect to a MailChimp API, and reference your campaign IDs column to bring latest data accurately (opens, clicks, bounces, replies, etc.), without having the need to individually track your campaigns or do manual data analysis.

4. Plan Your Video Production and Track Your Video Campaigns with YouTube Integration

Demand for video content is growing and 87% of marketers are using video as a marketing channel to increase their brand awareness and sales while keeping the customers informed. 1.9 billion logged in users visit YouTube every month and they watch a billion hours of video EVERY DAY. With YouTube, also being the second most visited site on the web after Google, you cannot miss this as a marketing channel in today's time.

Use Stackby to manage your video production planning. Connect your column to a YouTube API and reference your YouTube video IDs to bring all the details in a single click, whether content (Title, Duration, etc.) or stats (Views, Likes, Comments, Dislikes, etc.), and keep refreshing to bring in the latest information.

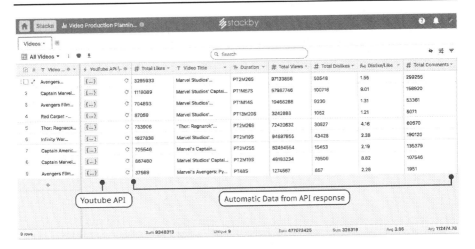

Not just that, you can also track your competitor's videos by tracking their metrics and correlate it to yours on how you can optimize your next video campaign.

5. Measure Your Web pages Performance with Google PageSpeed

With better SEO efforts, you can increase your website's visibility and rankings. Google is responsible for 94% of total organic traffic and organic SEO is 5.66x better than paid search ads. That's why 61% marketers say improving SEO and growing organic presence is their top inbound marketing priority.

Stackby helps you track your website performance by connecting your column to a Google PageSpeed API and referencing your web page URLs to bring in all the details in a single actionable table. These include Performance audits (Loading, Latency), SEO audits (Meta Description, Canonical, Robot.txt), Accessibility, Best Practices, etc.

Keep implementing your suggestions and track metrics by refreshing your data, no manual data entry.

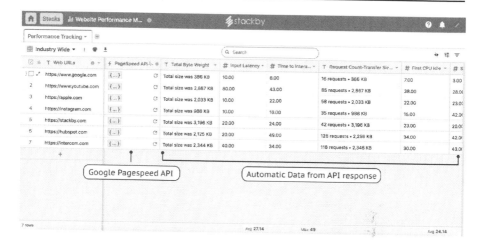

6. Learn, Iterate and Repeat

It's important to finally learn from these metrics and summarize the results and knowledge into your various campaigns to make them more effective.

As you become better in the process, you can plan, measure and track your metrics to grow your services.

In today's world when time means money and every aspect of growth hacking is dependent on how much faster you reach your goals, Stackby helps you do just that by bringing everything on to a single canvas with multiple API integrations.

It's simply easier for you to manage your entire process with just a few clicks, in the shortest time possible. No more manual entries for generating lead lists or analytics data. Automating your processes is the key to growth hacking, and that's how it democratizes the growth hacking experiments for everyone, regardless of their technical skills.

Free trial of Stackby

www.stackby.com/signup or

choose one of the predefined templates at

www.stackby.com/templates to manage and automate your various growth experiments.

Stackby is a collaborative database platform that empowers end users to create their own workflows and automate it via third party services. It brings together the familiarity of spreadsheet-style interface, functionality of databases and best business APIs (YouTube, MailChimp, Clearbit, etc.) on a single new customizable canvas. No coding and training needed.

AUTHOR BIOGRAPHY

Rachit Khator is the Founder and CEO of Stackby.com, a collaborative database platform that helps non-technical people create and customize their own software. Before Stackby, he spent 4 years working in Venture Capital and Product Management for a large Fortune 500 in Michigan, USA, where he led investments and worked with over 15+ technology startups, and was part of a few successful multi-million $ exits.

He holds dual Master's degrees in Applied Physics from NIT Surat, India and in Entrepreneurship from the University of Michigan, Ann Arbor. He returned to India in 2018 to build Stackby, after years of struggle in dealing with multiple spreadsheets and applications.

Where to Find Rachit
www.stackby.com
www.www.facebook.com/stackby
www.twitter.com/StackbyHQ
www.linkedin.com/company/relytree

"Google is responsible for 94% of total organic traffic and organic SEO is 5.66x better than paid search ads. That's why 61% marketers say improving SEO and growing organic presence is their top inbound marketing priority."

WHY PARTNERSHIPS ARE THE ULTIMATE GROWTH HACK

By Naser Alubaidi

In the marketing world, 'growth hacking' is probably the most misused and overused buzzword of all time.

Everyone is looking for that one hack, that one win that'll solve all their growth problems.

The sad reality however, is that there are no magic bullets when it comes to growth. A magic button color or an exit pop-up is simply not going to cut it.

Real growth is sustainable. Real growth is also scalable. Real growth is a mindset. Most importantly, real growth is a process, a hypothesis-driven iterative process for everything you do; from developing new ideas, to reaching a new audience and finding product-market fit.

Growth comes from winning a thousand tiny battles, not one quick 'hack,' and partnerships are the best way to accelerate the process of winning these battles, with the result of accelerating growth.

Before we jump into how you can use partnerships to hack your growth, let's start by looking at the most important part of your strategy: your ultimate goal.

I like to use an analogy here, which I learned from author, David Deida. David compares life to an onion. He says, "at the core of the onion is every person's ultimate purpose or goal in life, and to reach your goal, you need to align EVERYTHING in your life to that onion: diet, friends, career, network etc. and by doing so, you slowly peel layer after layer of that onion which brings you closer and closer to your ultimate goal."

In a lot of ways, growth operates in exactly the same way. Let's call it the 'Growth Onion'.

At the core of that 'Growth Onion' is YOUR ultimate business goal and to reach that goal, you will have to align ALL your strategies and experiments with it. There are no 'one-size-fits-all' goals when it comes to growth. Your goal will depend primarily on the nature of your business, the stage you're at and what you are trying to achieve.

The key is to choose a goal that is specific enough to allow you to align everything to it, and general enough that you'll be able to pivot as you experiment and test different strategies.

Once you have your goal set in stone, it's time to shift to how you can use partnerships to hack your growth.

"At the core of that 'Growth Onion' is YOUR ultimate business goal and to reach that goal, you will have to align ALL your strategies and experiments with it." #TheGrowthHackingBook #GrowthHackingMovement #GrowthHackingDay

Why Partnerships are the 'Ultimate Growth Hack'

I have to admit, I also fell victim to the lucrative promises of growth hacking, desperately searching for that one hack that'll solve all our growth problems. I kept searching and trying.

I tested tens, if not hundreds of growth hacks, from SEO hacks, getting reviews on G2Crowd and Capterra, exit popup hacks, gamification, pop-ups, viral loops and various tactics other marketers raved about.

Some of these tactics did actually work temporarily but quickly proved not to be scalable and sustainable or simply weren't good enough.

The problem was, we didn't have the customers, the revenue, the brand, or even the network. Nobody knew who we were.

That's exactly why partnerships were perfect for us. Not only did they help us get exposure and generate leads we needed in the short-term, they also influenced our growth in so many different ways:

- Gave us the social proof we needed.
- Helped set us up as thought-leaders in our niche.
- Expanded our access to a broader audience and a new audience.
- Provided more exposure, which resulted in better partners.

Thankfully, I was able to successfully duplicate the same partnership tactics we used in different SaaS startups, all who needed to grow very quickly and didn't have the budget to do so.

The secret is the compounding nature of partnerships.

The 'Partnership Compounding Cycle'

In the finance world, compounding is the process whereby an asset generates earnings, which are reinvested to generate their own earnings. With compound interest, the longer you invest your money, the higher your earnings are going to be every year.

In the marketing world, we found that partnerships have a nature similar to 'compound interest', which is exactly what makes partnerships the ultimate growth hack.

The compounding cycle of partnerships goes something like this:

1. You partner up with Company X.
2. This partnership gives you access to Company X's audience.
3. You nurture those leads and turn them into users.
4. The exposure and association with Company X help build your brand's credibility.
5. The credibility you built helps you attract better partners.
6. Repeat.

Simply put, the more partnerships you have, the more exposure you'll get, the more users and more social proof you'll have and as a result, you are able to partner with better brands for better exposure, and the cycle goes on and on.

Choosing the right partners

It's important to note there is no "one-size-fits-all" manual for partnerships however, there are a few questions you can ask yourself to identify who the right partners are for you:

1. Do they have a similar type of audience to what my company has and wants to grow?
2. Is there a competitive overlap, are we offering the same services or targeting the same keywords?
3. How many leads am I getting from this partnership and is the number large enough to be worth my time?
4. Does this brand have a good reputation?
5. Are the people you're working with enjoyable to work with?

These questions will help you identify if a certain brand or company is the right partner for you. They are likely to be a great partner if they:

1. Are an established brand in their industry
2. Share a similar audience
3. Are not a competitor
4. Have a sizeable audience: email list, social following, etc.
5. Seem easy to work with and flexible

You may to settle for smaller partners if your startup is at an early stage and as you keep this cycle going, before you know it, your partners will quickly become the biggest names in the industry.

Types of Partnerships to Leverage

The type of partnership you choose depends primarily on the product offering and audiences you and your partner have.

In the case of 'Supreme,' co-branded clothes and accessories make the most sense for them and their partners.

As a SaaS startup, we found the three types of partnerships that make the most sense for us are:

1. Content Partnerships and Co-marketing
2. Link Building Partnerships
3. Strategic Partnerships

1) Content Partnerships / Co-marketing

Co-marketing partnerships are when two or more companies work together to promote a shared offer, usually a co-branded piece of content. This is very similar to Supreme's "co-branding" partnerships.

There are various different types of co-marketing projects you could work on, but the most notable ones are:

- eBooks
- Webinars
- Joint-Research

- Video Series
- Newsletter Swaps
- Any other co-branded pieces of content

With these projects, the goal is to establish mutually beneficial partnerships that generate leads and add value to all parties involved by pooling resources and expertise, to write a piece of content that resonates with both your audience and your partners' audience.

In many cases, we found this type of partnership, to be the beginning of a long-term relationship with that brand. The key is to choose the right partner and to add as much value to them as possible.

By proving the value of partnerships to your partner and showing them your ability to deliver on a promise, they are more likely to expand your partnership in the future.

2) Link Building Partnerships

Link building is the process of getting external websites to link back to your website. Building backlinks to your pages has two main benefits:

1. Helps drive referral traffic to your website
2. Increases your site's authority (which helps you rank higher on Google).

This process remains a vital factor in how search engines determine which pages rank on every keyword. As a result, the more backlinks you have from quality websites, the more likely you are to earn higher rankings on Google.

Link building partnerships can exist in a variety of ways, we'll look at the three main ways we have built links to all of our blog posts and pages, i.e. Home page and landing pages.

a) **Link Exchanges (not recommended):** This is probably the most popular link building strategy used by online companies and blogs. It is a quick and simple collaboration where you add a link to your partner's page in an existing blog post and in return, they would add a link to one of your pages on their website.

Even though this tactic still seems to work well, it does come with the risk of being penalized by Google if done too often.

b) **Guest Posting:** This is pretty much self-explanatory. You approach an authority blog in your industry and offer to write a guest post for their blog. Guest blogging gives you the opportunity to build your authority and your brand's authority.

The blogs you write with are usually okay with you adding a link to your homepage in the author bio section. Also, in most cases, you are able to fit a few backlinks to relevant blog posts or your pages in the post itself.

A way we 'hacked' this was to find different bloggers in the industry who are doing guest posting themselves and simply asked them to share a list of all the pages they are trying to build links to. This was so we can start including links to these partners whenever we're writing a guest post on an external website, and naturally, they would do the same with us.

Now, in every guest post we write, not only do we include a link to our pages, but also six or seven links to our partners. As a result, we get around seven or eight links, on different websites, for every guest post we write. Easy, right?

c) **The Guestographic Method:** This is my favorite approach. This is a link building technique which uses infographics in a new way. With this method, you simply create an infographic on your site, find blogs that cover the same topic, share your infographic with them and see if they would be interested in adding it to one of their blog posts.

You can also offer to write a mini-blog post, which will include the infographic. Here, you are adding value to your partners by offering them something tangible versus simply asking them for a link. You are more likely to be successful using this method.

We took this strategy to the next level by offering to summarize long blog posts on external websites with an infographic, in exchange for a link to one of our blog posts. In that case, we ask them to provide us with an outline and we quickly create an infographic that has their content on it.

Link building partnerships are usually quicker than co-marketing projects, but their effectiveness is also much smaller. However, the way we approach this partnership is exactly the same as any other type: it's simply an opportunity to build a long-term relationship with these brands and expand our partnerships further.

3) Strategic Partnerships

This brings us to the last type of partnership that could help you hack your growth. This includes any type of mutually beneficial partnerships you can create with other companies in your industry. The three main types of strategic partnerships we executed successfully in the past are:

a) Integrations

We mentioned Airbnb's integration with Craigslist earlier in this post and how it helped them hack their growth. Integrations are a great way for companies to expand their product's offerings and improve customer experience significantly.

b) Affiliates

Affiliate marketing is a great way to partner up with customers who love you and enjoy your product the most. By compensating them for referrals, you are allowing users to become evangelists for your product.

Similarly, partnering up with influencers and brands in your industry and compensating them for their recommendations is a great way to drive more traffic & sales to your business.

c) Marketing/Publicity Stunts

This is probably the toughest type of partnership to execute on, but it's a game-changer when done right. Most marketers often overlook collaborating with other brands with the goal to go viral or execute on a marketing stunt. Not only does this reduce your potential cost by half, it also doubles your chances of successfully executing on your viral campaign.

Of course, there are many other partnership types that could be right for your business. However, I only mentioned the ones we personally tested and successfully executed on in the past few years.

Conclusion

Growth is a step-by-step process. Achieving sustainable and scalable growth is the result of hundreds of tiny experiments, optimizations and hacks.

Creating partnerships however, can help you accelerate your growth by leveraging their powerful compounding nature. The more partnerships you have, the higher the effectiveness of each partnership is going to be to your business growth.

Whether you're looking to build your user base, build your brand or simply increase your profits, partnerships are a sure way to influence every single factor around your business and skyrocket your growth.

AUTHOR BIOGRAPHY

Naser Alubaidi is the Growth Lead at Venngage, a leading graphic design platform. He worked with several early-stage startups where he implemented a growth strategy centered on partnerships.

Naser currently leads partnerships at Venngage and has helped grow their user base to millions of users worldwide. He has successfully partnered with hundreds of companies over the last few years including HubSpot, Vimeo and other industry leaders.

Where to Find Naser
www.linkedin.com/in/naseralubaidi

"We took this strategy to the next level by offering to summarize long blog posts on external websites with an infographic, in exchange for a link to one of our blog posts. In that case, we ask them to provide us with an outline and we quickly create an infographic that has their content on it."

How To Market Your Business Like A Reality Tv Show: Harnessing The Power Of Storytelling To Make Money And Grow Your Business

By Tim Wasmundt

I've worked in Hollywood for the last 15 years on some of the biggest reality shows to date, and I've created shows around businesses that have made them millions of dollars and brought invaluable recognition to their brand.

To some, I'm considered an expert in the art of storytelling. Now, I've taken the things I've learned working in the industry and created something I call 'Branded Storytelling.' I view it as the ultimate tool to set businesses apart from their competition. Let me explain.

If you have a business or a brand, then you probably understand that in order for you to be successful, grow your business and make more money, you need to get you and your product and services into the minds of your potential customers. You've got to find a way to connect to your potential customers.

Seems obvious - right? Yes, but with the influx and oversaturation of ads and commercials, that connection is getting harder and harder to make.

What if you could get noticed by people and turn them into raving fans, by telling your story? You see, the amazing thing is, raving fans will do your marketing for you.

The best way to connect to people is through storytelling

Since the beginning of human existence, we've told stories. From cave drawings, to campfire tales, to moving pictures, we've always told stories. At their very core, good stories share the same basic themes and characteristics, a hero, trying to accomplish something and a 'bad guy' trying to stop the hero from succeeding.

As the audience, we sit totally engaged and on the edge of our seats wondering what will happen next. Will the guy or girl find their love? Will the hero's team win the game? These stories have the power to hold our attention, they have the power to elicit emotion and they bring the audience along on a journey.

Here's the secret for building your business: If you can turn your message into a story and tell it in an entertaining way, you can hook your audience and take them on your journey. The ability to do this requires a connection, which means you've successfully engaged people. Engaging and connecting will make people interested and that turns your audience members into customers.

Hollywood, and the film and television industry figured this out a long time ago. They use the power of storytelling to entertain, and ultimately to sell their viewers something in the process. 'Show business' is just that — a business, which ultimately has to sell something, whether it's a ticket to the movie theater or a product on screen or in a commercial between shows.

You see, people in general have this feeling that, "if it's on the screen, it must be cool and I want to be a part of it." This is why product placement in films and television has been going on forever. As consumers we want to wear what celebrities and actors wear, what they eat and drink, what they do, and so on. Reality TV is no different and to some extent, it has an even greater power to influence its viewers, because of the 'real factor' that viewers perceive and the connection they feel to the reality TV stars.

"Here's the secret for building your business: If you can turn your message into a story and tell it in an entertaining way, you can hook your audience and take them on your journey." #TheGrowthHackingBook #GrowthHackingMovement #GrowthHackingDay

After working in reality TV for years and seeing businesses grow in revenue, sales and brand recognition, from the exposure they received, a light bulb went off. I realized that by creating reality shows FOR businesses and brands, instead of for a television network or movie studio, it would allow for the people behind the business to tell their own authentic story, instead of 'Hollywood' dictating the story. When told in an entertaining and compelling way, these shows and stories have the ability to evoke an emotional connection and in turn attract an audience who are interested in your business and who want to follow along and to be a part of your story. When done right, storytelling is THE ultimate tool to driving your success.

After discovering the power of storytelling for businesses, I knew it was time to put our 'Branded Storytelling' concept to work by creating entertaining content and web series for businesses and brands. In 2014, I started Von Skye Original, an award winning Production Company that produces premium story driven content for businesses, brands and anyone else trying to tell their story. It was a major pivot in business practices for me, since up to that point I had been creating content for TV networks. To be honest, it was a little scary but I believed in the 'Branded Storytelling' concept and knew it was the right thing to do.

In 2015, a friend of mine introduced me to Michael Ungaro, the CEO of San Pedro Fish Market, one of the largest restaurants in the country. His family has owned and operated the market since the late 1950's and they were looking to reinvent their marketing and drive new business. This was the perfect opportunity to use 'Branded Storytelling' to innovate for the San Pedro Fish Market. That's when we created *Kings of Fi$h*, a reality show about the families who own and operate the Fish Market.

With my years of experience producing, directing and editing network TV, I used my storytelling abilities to weave the San Pedro Fish Market narrative with the business as the backbone, into authentic, compelling and entertaining stories. People started to pay attention and they began to follow the 'Kings' story. As their audience began to grow, so did the business — literally! The series has been a huge marketing tool, they've seen their revenue go up 20% since we started it. As one of the largest restaurants in the country, that's no small change. They've even expanded and opened three new locations, with a fourth on the way. We have produced 50 episodes so far, with two spin-offs and over 120 million views on social media. The business is the backbone of the series, but we definitely have fun with the stories and characters. We've had a wide variety of storylines in the past six seasons.

As *Kings Of Fi$h* became more successful, a cool by-product began to happen, the series itself became a brand, with branded merchandise and live events presented by *Kings Of Fi$h*. The series also runs on televisions at all San Pedro Fish Market restaurant locations. We look forward to continuing to grow the *Kings Of Fi$h* brand and see where their story goes next.

The Von Skye Original story is growing too. With many other shows and projects in the works, it's just the beginning for the 'Branded Storytelling' concept. Whether you're a business or 'personality' looking to tell your story and build your brand or an agency looking to have the edge on your competition, by providing premium story driven content, our 'Branded Storytelling' is the way to go. If you're ever in need of story consulting or even a full production company, my team of skilled and seasoned producers has you covered. I'm confident that our storytelling expertise can not only help to bring out your best story, but to also get it out to the world. I have used the power of storytelling to change businesses and lives. When used properly, it really is that powerful of a tool. I can't wait to tell the next greatest story. Could it be yours?

Now that I've shared parts of my story and my journey, I want to share some insider information on how you can start harnessing the power of story:

Harness the power of a Hollywood Story Team

Story is king, so develop the most compelling story and clear message around your business. Find the best characters — whether it's the motivated entrepreneur, the quirky and fun employees or the customers themselves, it's important to find people who are interesting to watch, as you guide viewers through your story.

It's also very important and this may be the hardest part, to find the perfect balance between being entertaining and compelling, while conveying the narrative of your business. If you miss that balance, your goal of turning the viewers into customers and fans will not be reached. It'll either be, just another fun thing to watch or a commercial, and neither of those will truly set you apart. At the very least, I suggest finding someone who you can consult with during this initial story and messaging process.

Harness the power of a Hollywood TV Production Company, or take a production course at the very least

There has never been a better time to create content, but that's the case for everyone, so find ways to set yourself apart. While story trumps production value (you could shoot it all on an iPhone if your story was compelling enough), your content should look and feel big, and this will give you an edge on your competition.

Fill your social channels and websites with **television network quality** content that is entertaining and clearly conveys your message. Working with Von Skye Original will allow you to harness the power of a Hollywood production company for budgets that fit any size business.

Harness the power of Innovative Technology

Television or traditional television is on its way out and the digital platform is taking over. People engage with content differently now and the digital trend is on the rise. While this space is constantly changing, intrinsic storytelling and the need to tell stories will never go away. Today, thanks to technology, there are a multitude of options and ways to deliver our stories.

To be a leader in your industry you need to have your 'finger on the pulse' of how your audience is consuming content and you need to be innovative in getting your message across. Engaging your audience with your story is the key. The story format (reality, documentary or scripted) is dependent upon your intended message and goals. Take advantage of digital platforms to give you an edge, to reach the most people and turn your brand into something that 'everyone' is talking about.

Good luck in finding ways to grow your business, that's part of this journey. Tell your story and people will follow.

AUTHOR BIOGRAPHY

Tim Wasmundt is an Executive with over 15 years of Hollywood industry experience as a Producer, Editor and Director. He is an expert storyteller, dedicated to creating authentic, entertaining, compelling and innovative multi-platform content.

Tim's award winning production company, **Von Skye Original** specializes in premium, authentic story driven content. Tim is an Industry leader, with a keen understanding of the marketplace and the powerful connection between telling stories and growing successful businesses and brands.

Where to Find Tim
Website : storyboss.tv
Instagram: @storybosstv // @kingsoffish
Facebook: @vonskyeoriginal // @KingsOfFish
Twitter: @vonskyeoriginal
Podcast: The Story Boss (iTunes)

"Story is king, so develop the most compelling story and clear message around your business. Find the best characters — whether it's the motivated entrepreneur, the quirky and fun employees or the customers themselves, it's important to find people who are interesting to watch, as you guide viewers through your story."

GROWTH HACKS TO GENERATE A FLOOD OF LEADS, CUSTOMERS AND PROFITS (WITHOUT PAID ADS)

By Rohan Chaubey and Amit Kumar

How will you act if I told you it is impossible to fail?

The growth hacks mentioned in this chapter are battle-tested and lesser-known. I use these growth hacks to grow my own business and my clients.

It is impossible for your startup to fail if you apply this new knowledge.

We encourage you to take action on this information to build a scalable lead generation machine for your product or agency or consultancy.

The growth hacks shared in this chapter will allow you to quickly become the undisputed leader in your chosen industry, and drive many leads and growth opportunities.

Growth Hack Title: Upsell and Cross-Sell Building Complementary Tools

Short Description: Get a ton of inbound leads for your product or service by building complementary SaaS tools or software.

Difficulty Level: Advanced

Effectiveness: ★★★★★

Goal: Have you noticed how some SaaS companies are actually running an agency in disguise by upselling or cross-selling their services? You can get an avalanche of leads for your agency services by offering a complementary free or freemium tool.

Time to Implement: 2 days to several weeks (depends on what you are building)

What You'll Need: An idea for the tool and an in-house or freelance developer

Description/Overview: This growth hack will earn you more leads than you ever thought possible. Of course, you will have to invest in building a free or freemium tool, but the ROI will be far greater than your initial investment. Freemium tools also get a lot of free PR and coverage on blogs and publications.

I developed a freemium platform that helped users skyrocket their Twitter engagement and make their tweets go viral. It helped me attract 1200+ qualified leads organically within 3 months. My upsell service was Twitter organic targeted followers growth. Listing a few reputed organizations that signed up on my platform: UBER, UNESCO, Candere by Kalyan Jewellers, Stuhrling, FreshChat, BBN Times, and 1200+ more.

You can cross-sell and upsell your agency services to the people who're signing up for your freemium product. Also, you can create a new revenue stream for yourself by introducing 'Land and Expand' freemium pricing model to your tool.

Step-by-Step Process:

Action item #1

First, you'll need to come up with a product idea.

It shouldn't be a vitamin, it should be a painkiller. In other words, it shouldn't be a "nice-to-have" tool, it should be a "must-have" tool.

Recognize some hot-button issues in your niche. Check if that product idea complements the services that you want to be a recognized expert for. Go with that. It should be something that hasn't already been developed or must be better than all the existing solutions.

Perhaps, you can develop a product that solves your own problems related to a particular business function in your niche. Most probably other people in your industry are also frustrated about the same problem.

Action item #2

Once you have a product idea, talk to developers in your team or hire agencies or freelance developers who can help you figure if it is technically feasible to build it.

The product can be a web app, chrome extension, mobile app or a desktop app.

Build an MVP. You have to keep the development costs low as this tool is just complementary to your services. Think of it as a lead magnet.

Based on my experience, it is much cheaper to build chrome extensions and desktop apps. But web apps gain a lot of traction.

Build a helpful functional tool that establishes trust to your brand and the users will eventually pay for your complementary services.

Action item #3

Build apps so valuable that businesses have no choice but to see it as the ultimate solution to their problem, no matter how small is the problem that you are trying to solve.

In 2017, I built a Pinterest growth chrome extension because there were no free and reliable growth tools for Pinterest.

In 2018, I developed a SaaS platform that guaranteed virality on Twitter.

Our definition of virality was ranking on the top tweets page on Twitter under specific hashtags. In other words, being seen by people outside of your immediate network.

In 2019, a desktop app I launched acts as an interface between Instagram and the user. It helps the user get email and phone numbers of their prospects or influencers on Instagram from a pool of 25 million publicly listed contacts.

The table below lists the products I have built so far and the ROI based on my initial investment.

29X ROI means, I made 29 times more money than the initial amount I invested.

For example, If a product costs $3500 to develop and maintain, 29X ROI suggests you made $101500 out of it. This is achieved either by selling a subscription to the product or by cross-selling your services to the leads you acquire through the product.

Use Case	Product Type	Cross-Sell Offer	ROI
Pinterest Growth	Chrome Extension	Social Media Organic Growth and Management Services	2X
Twitter Virality	SaaS App	Social Media Organic Growth and Management Services	4X
Lead Generation from Instagram	Desktop App	Full-Stack Growth Marketing Service	29X

Case Study:

SocialBee.io is a fantastic example of using this growth hack. With their software widely loved by the small businesses and social media marketers, many don't even realize that SocialBee is more than just a social media management tool. They also offer social media and content services.

Conclusion/Summary: Now you have actionable steps that can help you get free leads worth thousands of dollars for your product or services. Apply your new knowledge.

By Social Animal

Growth Hack to Create Content Your Audience Will Love, Gain More Relevant Traffic From Social Media, and Exponentially Increase Your Content Marketing Engagement

The following growth hack is an upgrade to the existing content marketing techniques and it reduces manual effort by 80%.

The techniques for content growth shared in this chapter will make you one of the most influential content marketers in your chosen niche, and drive more engagement, and business opportunities.

Growth Hack Title: 10X your content marketing ROI

Short Description: Increase your content marketing engagement exponentially to market to your best audience

Difficulty Level: Medium

Effectiveness: ★★★★★

Goal: To increase content marketing engagement exponentially by creating exceptional content, growing social media following, partnering with the best influencers with no paid promotion

Time to Implement: A few hours!

What You'll Need: A subscription to Social Animal and an understanding of how the use the data.

Description/Overview: This growth hack will 10X your content marketing ROI which might take years for your competitors.

You will have to subscribe to at least the basic version of Social Animal to use this hack at its maximum potential.

Using these techniques, you can exponentially grow your Twitter engagement and make your content go viral.

Not just that, you will make your blog achieve targets which might have been impossible at a time.

Step-by-Step Process:

Action item 1 - Audience Research

Knowing your audience is an essential and significant step when you decide to create a content marketing strategy that decides your ROI.

Audience research tells you what kind of content you must create, and where you must share it to reach the maximum number of people.

Social Animal's "Article search" lets you browse through thousands of articles that have gained top shares over any period for any keyword.

You can also analyze your competitor's articles to see which post has got maximum engagement and see which social media platform works best for the type of content you create.

Action Item 2 - Content Creation

You'll need to know what to create, when to create and how to create.

Analyzing top shared articles and their headlines plus their word counts would give you a fair idea.

Social Animal helps you analyze, draw data and construct a helpful strategy by telling you what works best.

This way you have a perfect portrait of the necessary elements on your hands, which can make your content stand out from the crowd.

In the articles section, find the most shared articles for your target keyword and know the data points to focus on by moving to the insights menu.

Action Item 3 - Competitor research

Collecting and reviewing information about rivals is crucial.

Analyzing your competitors provides the best defensive strategy, also enabling you to copy or mimic what they do after concluding what works best for them.

Monitor your competitors and track their mentions every day using Social Animal dashboard.

Analyze their content and get useful insights like the average title length of their articles, their average engagement rate, their best day to post, and the social media platform.

This gives you the best knowledge of your potential audience and this actionable data helps you to take measures right away.

Action Item 4 - Review and analyze content performance

Where do you stand in terms of content generation and engagement?

Have you ever assessed or scrutinized your domain by comparing your content marketing data with a competitor's?

Find where and when you can do better with Social Animal's "Insights" section.

Action Item 5 - Content Curation

When it comes to social media, you must always be a step ahead.

You'll have to engage continuously with posts that attract a lot of audiences. And how do you find these attractive posts?

What sort of content do you curate? And which platform is best suited for you and your audience?

Social Animal answers all that and more. Just the keyword your audience like reading about and enter your target keyword in the article section.

You can find the most shared and most liked content on your keyword and then share it directly from the tool to any specific social media channel or even curate it using Buffer.

Action Item 6 - Content Distribution and Promotion

Every content marketer knows it's hard to distribute and promote content.

But what if you could find people who have already shared your content or content that is similar to yours?

Reaching out to these people with a valuable article and getting them to readily share your content is the best thing that can boost your ROI.

The Influencers feature in Social Animal lets you find people based on what they share. Sort them through various filters and try hitting them up with a message. You'd be surprised by the number of responses you get.

Action Item 7 - Content Monitoring

Millions of articles are published and shared every day.

Along with the laser-sharp focus on your content, it is excellent to keep an eye on competitor's articles.

Don't you agree?

Here is how easy it is to monitor any keyword/competitor's content online.

Create a project by typing in keywords and your competitors in the Social Animal dashboard.

The tool's dashboard will display them all and you also get an email alert every day with a choice of top articles that mention your keywords and competitors.

Objective	Feature	Use case	ROI
Content creation, content curation	Articles	Find top shared articles, analyze headlines	4X
Competitor research	Insights	Find what works for your competitors, and an analysis of their content	8X
Influencer Marketing, Content promotion	Influencers	Partner with the best influencers for your brands, find micro influencers too!	10X

Case Study:

80% of marketers use engagement as their primary success metric.

A famous fashion brand used Social Animal to analyze it's competition and found the kinds of content they must create and how they must promote it.

They saw a 20% increase in engagement on their social media pages with a 12% increase in clicks to their website from social media platforms.

Their articles also saw a significant rise in rankings on Google.

Conclusion/Summary:

Once you start pumping out content, don't forget to access your content metrics.

Evaluate and find what's working. Create a content calendar that contains what you've done so far to execute your strategy more efficiently.

Company: Audiense + FindThatLead

Author: Rohan Chaubey

Use Twitter to Build An Outreach List

Growth Hack Title: Find Email Address Of Anyone On Twitter

Short Description: Find the email address of any Twitter account using Audiense + FindThatLead

Difficulty Level: Intermediate

Effectiveness: ★★★★

Goal: Create a process to identify targeted Twitter profiles and collect their email addresses.

Time to Implement: Less than 15 minutes

What You'll Need: Twitter account and an upgraded account on audiense.com and FindThatLead.com.

Description/Overview: Growing a targeted following on Twitter does not require running paid ads if you use Audiense.com. You can define your audience and engage with them via Audiense.

Who will benefit from finding email addresses of their Twitter followers or anyone on Twitter?

- Bloggers
- Journalists
- PR professionals
- B2B startups
- Marketing agencies, etc.

Step-by-Step Process:

Step 1: Find targeted Twitter profiles using Audiense

- Competitor's followers
- Followers from a specific geographic region
- Keyword search

Audiense has many other filters to find your niche audience.

Step 2: Export their names and website URLs

Audiense will allow you to export all the profile details. From the downloaded CSV file you only need names and website URLs.

Step 3: Use their website address and first name + last name to find email addresses using FindThatLead.

Upload the CSV on Findthatlead.com. FindThatLead will provide you all the email addresses you need.

Step 4: Verify email addresses

To make sure you do not send any emails to invalid emails or spam traps, verify the email addresses before sending them an email.

Step 5: You can send your email campaign using FindThatLead.

Please do not spam. Send creative and personalized outreach emails. :)

Conclusion/Summary: Now you can find the email addresses of bloggers, journalists and prospects on Twitter. Happy pitching!

Company Biographies

Social Animal is a top-notch content research and social analytics software which uses NLP and machine learning techniques to find top shared content, analyze trending articles, and find the most relevant influencers for your target keyword/domain.

Sign up here: SocialAnimal.com

(Use **GROWTHBOOK** coupon code to get 10% lifetime discount on all Social Animal plans).

Audiense is #1 Twitter Marketing Platform - Identify relevant audiences, discover actionable insights and inform your strategies to grow your business.

Sign up here: Audiense.com

FindThatLead is a B2B lead generation tool that finds and validates your future best customer's email in seconds. FindThatLead scales your lead generation for sales and growth.

Sign up here: FindThatLead.com

AUTHOR BIOGRAPHIES

Amit Kumar has around 8 years of experience and has worked in leading startups and enterprises in the leadership position. He has mastered the art of building a world-class team from scratch and deliver some critical consumer product.

He was also in the core team of a startup Dazo which got funded by Google India head and Amazon India head. He works at the intersection of technology, marketing, and product with a single goal to solve the complex business problems at scale.

Currently, he is the CEO of Rejolut which aims at disrupting technology consulting industry. Rejolut is an award-winning company specializing in building innovative digital products for fast-moving companies. It started with the mission "You have the vision, we have the execution" by the industry veterans who have around decades of experience working in startups and enterprise. Rejolut is working in the emerging tech like ML/AI, IoT, Blockchain, RPA and AR/VR.

Where to Find Amit
rejolut.com
www.linkedin.com/in/amitkumaragrawal1
twitter.com/rejolut

Rohan Chaubey is one of the most followed Growth Hackers (according to Audiense.com - Twitter and IBM's partner product).

He has a proven track record of making content go viral on LinkedIn, Twitter, Instagram, Quora, etc. One of his SlideShares attracted 100000+ views within 12 hours, which shows his virality formula is not just limited to major social channels, but also on off-beat marketing channels and communities.

Rohan is a serial entrepreneur and SaaS founder. Rohan and his SaaS products have helped notable companies and organizations like UNESCO, UBER, BBN Times, RedBull, Candere by Kalyan Jewellers, Stuhrling, Congress, BJP, SoGoSurvey, Freshworks, Interesting Engineering, Quest Nutrition and many others.

He is also a speaker, business columnist and award-winning blogger. His articles and products have been featured on top-tier media publications including HuffPost, The Next Web, Forbes, Good Men Project and many other popular blogs/publications. He also had the honor of being listed as one of the 30 changemakers in India for the year 2018.

Rohan's growth marketing agency helps startups and companies unlock explosive, exponential, long-term growth using movement marketing, growth marketing services and growth tools.

Where to Find Rohan
Learn one new growth hack every day:
www.rohanchaubey.com
www.twitter.com/rohanchaubey4
www.linkedin.com/in/rohanchaubey1
www.instagram.com/rohanchaubey
www.youtube.com/rohanchaubeyy
www.quora.com/profile/Rohan-Chaubey

ABOUT THE PUBLISHER

GrowthMedia.AI is a cutting-edge business consulting platform, serving professionals who seek to reinvent themselves and leave a legacy. We offer turn-key business solutions - from idea to branding, from concept to success. We publish bestselling authors, we grow your tribe, we help you to become the expert authority in your field.

We offer comprehensive business analysis as well as mindset coaching. We have proudly published over 150 Bestselling Authors, built over 50 Sales Funnels and Membership Sites, and we already launched over 30 Social Media Campaigns. Our PR Campaigns have resulted in effective media mentions in CNBC, ABC, CBS, FOX, Forbes, Thrive Global, She Owns It, Mind Body Green, The WallStreet Journal and Huffington Post...

Our team is here to support your Message, and your Mission! Our company is an international business platform built to empower authentic leadership on the Planet. It's time for you to rise and make a difference!

We outsource and manage some of the most outstanding talents, across five continents, to brand your message, establish your authority and provide the best content for your audience and your ideal clients.

Whether you seek to rock on Instagram or YouTube, Facebook or Linkedin, our team is here to support you. Or, perhaps you'd like to launch a successful iTunes Podcast?

Awesome! Let's talk!
Parul Agrawal & Rohan Chaubey
Founders
www.growthmedia.ai

Made in the USA
San Bernardino, CA
24 July 2019